British Art

in the Victoria and Albert Museum

Michael Darby

Published in association with the
Victoria and Albert Museum

Scala/Philip Wilson

© 1983 Philip Wilson Publishers Ltd and
Summerfield Press Ltd

First published in 1983 by Philip Wilson
Publishers Ltd and Summerfield Press Ltd
Russell Chambers, Covent Garden,
London WC2E 8AA

Designed by Paul Sharp
Edited by Philip Wilson Publishers Ltd
Series Editor: Judy Spours

Produced by Scala Istituto Fotografico Editoriale, Firenze
Phototypeset by Tradespools Ltd, Frome, Somerset
Printed in Italy

ISBN 0-85667-112-6

Abbreviations:
D. = Depth
Diam. = Diameter
H. = Height
L. = Length
W. = Width

Frontispiece
The Victoria and Albert Museum: the main front,
designed by (Sir) Aston Webb in the 1890s.

Front cover
Miniature portrait of a lady called Frances, Countess of Somerset (1590–1632) by Isaac
Oliver (d. 1617)

Back cover
Stained glass designed by William Morris (1834–96)

Contents

British Art
in the Victoria and Albert
Museum

Introduction

Osterley House. Osterley was completed in 1577 for Sir Thomas Gresham, but altered by Robert Adam in 1761 for Francis Child. Adam's work, which is based primarily on Roman classical interior architecture, also included the furnishings, most of which survive intact.

The façades which the Victoria and Albert presents to the public, designed by (Sir) Aston Webb in the 1890s, give a beguiling sense of uniformity to the Museum, which is perpetuated in the main entrance hall and surrounding galleries. When one penetrates further, however, one becomes aware of odd changes of level, unhappy junctions between galleries and corridors, different constructional materials, and areas decorated with polychrome tiles, enamelled tin, or spirit fresco. It becomes apparent that the story of the Museum's architectural development is not as straightforward as it seems. When one also discovers that some of the curatorial departments are based on media, ceramics, textiles, and metalwork, for example, whilst the Indian and Far Eastern Departments are based on cultures and the Museum of Childhood and the Theatre Museum relate to activities, one's comprehension of the V & A is further confounded. That a decorative arts museum should house the national collection of water-colours and the Constable collection, which would seem more appropriate to the Tate or the National Galleries, complicates the issue still more.

The picture becomes clearer when one looks at the history of the Museum. The V & A came into being in the aftermath of the Great Exhibition of 1851, as the brain-child of the Prince Consort and of Henry Cole (1808–82), the principal promoters of the Crystal Palace. They were concerned about the low standard of design in British industry, and set out to establish not only the inseparability of art and manufacture, but also to expound the theory and practice of design in a simple, logical manner so as to make it comprehensible to manufacturers, designers, and public alike. This radical, utilitarian approach was reflected in the title of a new section of the Board of Trade called the Department of Practical Art (the forerunner of the present Department of Education and Science), which was set up in 1852 in Marlborough House with Cole as General Superintendent to administer both a museum and the metropolitan School of Design.

The Museum, called at first the Museum of Manufactures but renamed the Museum of Ornamental Art when it opened to the public in September 1852, initially comprised two quite separate collections. Some of the models, casts, and prints acquired for teaching purposes by the head school of design at Somerset House, including copies of Raphael's decorations of the Vatican Loggia and a miscellaneous collection of contemporary items purchased at the Paris Exhibitions of 1844 and 1845, were transferred to the Museum, and displayed alongside several hundred objects purchased at the Great Exhibition with the aid of a Government grant of £5,000 and a number of loans from the Royal and other prominent collections. The Museum immediately proved popular with the public, and it was not unusual for as many as 5,000 persons to visit Marlborough House when admission was free (6d entrance was otherwise charged).

The Museum's collections grew rapidly, and Cole could already boast by the end of 1853 of the ceramics, for example, that 'within its moderate compass there is probably no European collection more complete or comprehensive'. Under J. C. Robinson, whom Cole appointed as Superintendent of Art, the Bernal Collection of porcelain, maiolica, glass, and metalwork, and the Gherardini Collection of sculptors' models, including waxes attributed to Michaelangelo, were purchased in 1855. Important acquisitions were made at the Paris Exhibition in this year, and negotiations commenced for acquiring the large collection of medieval and Renaissance art belonging to the Toulouse lawyer, Jules Soulages.

With the intention of making the Museum more useful to the provinces and of encouraging the setting up of other museums throughout the country, a

Ham House. Originally built for Sir Thomas Vavasour, Ham House now stands as a monument to Elizabeth, Countess of Dysart, and her husband the Duke of Lauderdale. Recently restored, it is one of the most lavishly decorated and furnished seventeenth-century houses to have been preserved almost intact.

'Circulating Museum' of about four hundred objects was lent for study and exhibition to the provincial schools of art. This was later to become the Museum's Circulation Department. An expanding library of art books was also begun, which, like the Museum, was only open to the public on payment of a fee. Both Cole and Prince Albert were anxious that the Museum should, as far as possible, pay for its own running costs.

The difficulties of housing the collections and of providing adequate facilities for students was so acute by 1856 that Parliament agreed to transfer the entire Department to South Kensington. The Prince Consort succeeded in obtaining a vote from Parliament for £15,000, to which the Commissioners for the 1851 Exhibition added a further £3,000, and work was commenced on a 'temporary' corrugated and cast iron structure. The choice of site for the Department's move was perfectly logical because several years earlier the Prince had employed architects to plan a museum on the Commissioner's estate as part of a vast cultural centre, but the scheme had fallen through owing to lack of funds.

With the opening on 22 June 1857 of the 'Iron Museum', quickly renamed the 'Brompton Boilers' by the local inhabitants, who ridiculed its utilitarian appearance, began a new phase in the Department's history. The ground floor housed three quite different museums. The Educational Museum filled the major part, while the Museum of Ornamental Art under Robinson, and a Museum of Construction under the sapper-architect Francis Fowke, occupied

The Quadrangle. The northern side of the quadrangle was designed by Francis Fowke in 1863 and served for some time as the front entrance of the Museum. The pediment includes a mural commemorating the Great Exhibition of 1851.

smaller areas. Above these were situated several other museums and collections. The Architectural Museum was located in the western gallery, and included over 7,000 casts, principally of Gothic art. The eastern gallery contained the Museum of Animal Products, inherited from the 1851 Exhibition, and the popular food Museum arranged by Lyon Playfair, intended to provide 'lessons in household and health subjects, especially addressed to the working classes'. The northern gallery was given over to changing displays of recent work by members of the Institute of British Sculptors. Lastly, there was the collection of patent models administered by the Commissioners of Patents who objected to Cole's policy of charging for admission and had their own separate cottage-like entrance. Later, collections of marine models and of fish culture were added.

Thus, in this heterogeneous assemblage of Gothic casts and wax pork chops, of Renaissance sculpture and model boats, and of French furniture and stuffed animals, lay the ancestors of many modern institutions, including the Building and Design Centres, the National Maritime and Science Museums, and the Royal College of Art. Since John Sheepshanks had also given his collection of contemporary British art to the Department in 1856, the Tate Gallery could be added to the list. As the art collections continued to grow and space became more critical, so some of these collections were moved to new sites, and others disbanded; but the process was a long one, not completed until 1909 when those devoted to science were moved to the opposite side of Exhibition Road.

One of the conditions of the Sheepshanks gift was that a gallery should be erected to house the paintings within twelve months. The task of designing this was given to Francis Fowke, who had previously built a large refreshment room and photographic gallery elsewhere on the Department's site. When in 1859 the 'Iron Museum' was found 'unsuitable in every respect for the conservation of articles of value', many of the more precious objects were removed into the ground floor of the Sheepshanks Gallery. The Department's involvement with painting was given further impetus when one evening late in December 1856, while Cole was in Italy, Fowke was informed over dinner that they could begin a new building to house the Turner and Vernon collections (now in the National Gallery). To forestall bureaucratic interference Fowke began immediately, and these buildings continued the line of the Sheepshanks Gallery northwards, but formed an awkward junction with it, and were criticized on aesthetic grounds.

The collections of the Museum of Ornamental Art continued to grow. It must be remembered that in the first decade or so after the Department's foundation the Museum experienced little competition from other collectors. Art history as we know it today did not exist. A steady stream of important Renaissance and earlier works of art, such as would be inconceivable nowadays, flowed into the Museum: terra cottas and marbles by Donatello, Giambologna, and other Renaissance sculptors from the Gigli and Campana collections in 1860; the Gloucester candlestick from the Soltikoff Collection in the same year; the Eltenberg reliquary in 1861; the Syon Cope in 1864; the Raphael Cartoons on loan from the Queen in 1865; and hundreds of others.

By 1860 attendance had risen to more than 610,000 per annum and extra accommodation was again required for the collections. Cole rejected further piecemeal development and asked Fowke to draw up plans for major new buildings to incorporate or replace most of those already on the site. Building work was to last for more than twenty years and resulted in the appearance of much of the Museum as we know it today.

The Green Dining Room. This room, which was designed and decorated by Morris, Marshall, Faulkener and Company in 1863, was one of the first important commissions received by the firm, which quickly became famous for the production of textiles and wallpapers designed by its founder William Morris.

The Gamble Room. Like the Green Dining Room, the Gamble Room formed part of the original Museum restaurant. The ceramic columns and tiles were made by Minton, Hollins and Company of Stoke on Trent to the designs of Godfrey Sykes and James Gamble, and the room was opened in 1868.

In the decoration of the new buildings Fowke was helped by Godfrey Sykes, who clothed Fowke's ingenious architecture with 'the craftsmanship and humanist idealism of the Renaissance'. At the same time Cole called upon other artists, including Owen Jones, Morris and Company, E. J. Poynter, and Frederick Leighton, to carry out decorative work too. Thus, the Department took seriously its role as a promoter of practical art, many of the galleries becoming, as their decoration progressed, didactic displays of techniques and methods.

By this time the 'Iron Museum' was beginning to look decidedly out of place in its polychrome Renaissance setting, and in 1867 the greater part was removed and re-erected at Bethnal Green as the interior of what is now the Museum of Childhood. In its place two huge courts were built, from 1868, to house the collection of casts. Their completion in 1873 marked another turning-point in the history of the Museum. A new Chancellor of the Exchequer terminated the funds for building and thereby provoked Cole's resignation. 'South Kensington' as a whole may not have been Cole's inspiration, but many of the details were certainly his, and it was largely through his endeavour that it was achieved. What was not to Cole's liking was the bias of the collections towards art history. He blamed Robinson for this, and forced him to resign. Even after retirement Cole attempted to reverse the trend, but by 1880 his was a lone voice. The principles of good design he had formulated with Owen Jones and emblazoned on the gallery walls had long since been removed and the original purpose of the Museum forgotten.

The first major building work carried out after Cole's retirement was the completion in 1884 of the south side of the quadrangle containing the National Art Library. This was followed by the fronts to Cromwell and Exhibition Roads, which had been commenced when Queen Victoria laid the foundation stone in 1889, and were officially opened by King Edward VII in June 1909. It was at this time that the South Kensington Museum, as it had become known, was re-titled the Victoria and Albert Museum. In the present century, the story of development has largely been one of altering, hiding, or removing the Victorian features—now, happily, a policy that has been reversed—and of infill building to accommodate the growing collections.

Many major acquisitions were made in the later nineteenth century. The famous collection of English ceramics formed by Lady Charlotte Schreiber and presented in 1885, and John Jones' tremendously important bequest in 1882 of eighteenth-century French furniture and applied art, recently re-displayed in new galleries to the left of the main entrance, were two of the most important. Thousands of other gifts, purchases, and bequests have continued up to the present. The V & A has acquired a special niche in the hearts of many of its visitors. Dr W. L. Hildburgh, a wealthy American amateur scholar, gave presents to the Museum at Christmas and on his birthday, and quite apart from hundreds of important purchases over many years for most of the departments, bequeathed further enormous collections in 1956. Other very important acquisitions in the present century were Gabrielle Enthoven's theatre collection in 1925, one of the bases of the present Theatre Museum, and the purchases of the George Eumorphopoulous Collection in 1936, which with the collection of George Salting acquired in 1909 firmly established the importance of the Far-Eastern collections. Since responsibility for the India Office Museum had been assumed by the Department in 1879, the representation of Oriental art is now very strong. In 1947 and 1948 the contents of Ham and Osterley Houses were given to the

V & A, and in 1952 Apsley House, the home of the Duke of Wellington, also came into its care. These three out-stations are now administered by the Department of Furniture and Woodwork. As an indication of the numbers of objects presently entering the Museum's collections it is worth recording that more than 12,000 were received in 1978 alone.

The twentieth century has also seen the introduction of new departments in the Museum not specifically related to scholastic activities: the Conservation Department in 1960; Public Relations (now part of Museum Services) in 1964; the Design Section in 1968; Education in 1970; and the Exhibitions Section in 1975. Perhaps the most significant developments on the curatorial side to parallel these were the setting up of the Far Eastern Section in 1970, the confirmation of Bethnal Green as the Museum of Childhood in 1974, the closing of the Circulation Department in 1976, and the recognition of photography by its incorporation in the Department of Prints and Drawings, and Paintings in 1977. The establishment of the primary galleries after 1945 by the then Director, Sir Leigh Ashton, presented the greatest change in the public face of the Museum.

Ashton was fortunate to begin work with an almost empty building, for most of the collections had been moved to safety during the War. Present plans to redesign the primary galleries and include twentieth-century objects will not be achieved so easily. Indeed, there is the added problem now that much of the building is 'listed' and cannot, therefore, be altered. The cast courts have been successfully re-opened after a major programme of restoration, and the Department of Prints and Drawings, Paintings and Photographs has moved to the Henry Cole building (previously the Huxley building). It is to be hoped that it will not be long before a new restaurant opens in the basement of this building so that the present restaurant may be stripped out to reveal Sykes' brilliant South Court.

The long term is more difficult to assess. Decentralization for part of the collections must surely become necessary if the present rate of expansion continues. The artificiality of the barriers separating the V & A from the other national museums, in particular the Science and British Museums, is more than ever obvious. Even the practice of collecting in the art historical field (or is it the design field?) is being questioned. Art historians themselves point to the arbitrary nature of the present selection process, and social historians to many utilitarian and decorative objects not presently collected by the Museum, which popular consensus suggests deserve a place. Issues such as these have recently been brought sharply into focus by Sir Derek Rayner's report on the Museum. 'Devolution' from the Department of Education and Science, which he recommended, has resulted in the need to draw up specific aims and to accept wider financial responsibilities which have far-reaching implications for the public and private faces of the Museum.

Apsley House. The home of the Duke of Wellington, Apsley House was presented to the Nation in 1947. The house, which was originally designed by Robert Adam for Lord Bathurst, was much altered by Benjamin Dean Wyatt for the Duke of Wellington, who purchased it in 1817. It is situated at Hyde Park Corner.

Interior of the Museum of Childhood at Bethnal Green. The building first stood in South Kensington, where its utilitarian appearance caused it to be ridiculed as the 'Brompton Boilers'. It was moved to Bethnal Green in 1867 as a Museum of Science and Art for East London, and was recently re-named the Museum of Childhood.

The Shannongrove gorget Eighth century B.C.
This is one of some ten whole or fragmentary 'gorgets' or gold neck ornaments which come from the region of the Lower Shannon in Ireland. On the basis of similar gold ornaments found in the Gorteenreagh hoard, it can be dated to approximately the eighth century B.C. The workmanship is of an exceptional standard, and the method of joining the main sheet to the terminal discs by means of tabs and slots, and punched decoration, particularly interesting. Stylistically, the gorget probably owes as much to South West European influences as to Danish and West Baltic sources.

M.35–1948

Early Medieval and Gothic (to 1485)

In spite of its somewhat confused and arbitrary development, the Victoria and Albert Museum has succeeded in accumulating a collection of British art which now ranks as the finest in the world. Although this chapter opens with a consideration of some objects which are very early in date, it should be stressed that the Museum's interests, unlike those of the British Museum, are mainly post-medieval.

The Roman occupation of Britain ended during the first half of the fifth century, and with the Romans' departure classical art, which so depended on the stability and inherent knowledge of their leisured and cultured classes, departed too. What skills the Romans did leave behind were largely lost when new invaders from Northern Germany and Denmark fought their way into the country. When it did come, the revival in the arts was largely a result of the influence of Christianity: St Patrick's arrival in Ireland in 432 and St Augustine's in Canterbury in 597 both preceded periods of new creative activity. This was further encouraged by the Synod of Whitby in 663 and the re-establishment of links with a Roman world which was by that time heavily influenced by the Near East. Few British objects in the Museum's collection date from this period, and the seventh-century brooch illustrated here is secular. The ninth-century cross from Easby Abbey, near Richmond in Yorkshire depicts another form of Anglo-Saxon ornament. The carvings on the shaft are an elegant testimony to the birth of the art of sculpture in Britain.

Most of the objects displayed in Gallery 43 date from after the Norman conquest. The influx of northern-European Romanesque culture which followed Harold's defeat in 1066, however, did not exert as much influence in the decorative arts as it did in sculpture and architecture. Scrolling foliate forms with birds and biting beasts such as appear on the pectoral cross reliquary and the Gloucester candlestick owe far more to Saxon and Norse than to Norman, Carolingian, or Byzantine influences.

A single manuscript leaf from a Canterbury Psalter reminds us that it was in the workshops around the great schools of manuscript illumination associated with Canterbury and the cathedrals of St Albans, Winchester, and elsewhere that most of the ivories and metalwork displayed in the medieval galleries were made. One exception is the outstanding small whalebone relief of the Adoration of the Magi, which does not relate obviously to any particular school. Small-scale sculpture which could be easily carried was widely imported at this time, and although the relief is presently ascribed to a southern English workshop, it is quite possible that research will show it was carved on the Continent.

In 1174 a fire destroyed Canterbury cathedral, and during the next ten years it was rebuilt by William of Sens in the Gothic style of his native Île-de-France. As a result, Canterbury became the first major English building in the Gothic style which the Victorians called 'Early English'. Other cathedrals quickly followed, and as patrons demanded more elaborate and dramatic effects, so Gothic progressed through the 'Decorated' stage to its culmination in the 'Perpendicular' of the fourteenth and fifteenth centuries. Quite apart from the introduction of a new decorative and sculptural vocabulary, one effect of Gothic was to increase the size of windows, a great stimulus to stained glass designers.

While most English art and architecture at this time involved the importation of craftsmen and ideas from the Continent, the trend was different for English embroidery, *Opus Anglicanum*. Indeed, it has been said that no English artistic product has ever achieved wider fame than the embroidery of the Middle Ages.

The great Vatican inventory of 1295 lists far more pieces of *Opus Anglicanum* than any other type of embroidery. The bulk of this work was carried out in professional workshops, mostly situated in the City of London, and it involved not just the use of silk and silver-gilt thread, but also large quantities of pearls and precious stones, so that the finished pieces were often of immense value.

Superb embroidery had earlier been produced during the Anglo-Saxon period, such as the Bayeux Tapestry, but very few pieces have survived. All those displayed in the Museum date from after the Norman conquest. Perhaps the best-known are the fourteenth-century Syon and Butler-Bowden Copes and the thirteenth-century Clare Chasuble. All three, like the Jesse and Steeple Aston Copes shown in the same area, have been much altered, for like so many articles of Church property, *Opus Anglicanum* was refashioned or destroyed during the Reformation. Pieces still retaining their pearls and precious stones are almost non-existent, and much that has survived was preserved in the homes of Catholic families for occasional domestic use.

Of medieval gold and silversmith's work the Museum possesses several outstanding examples. The Gloucester candlestick is undoubtedly the best known. In the same case is a beautiful reliquary cross of *c.* 1000 made of gold with applied filigree work and plaques of cloisonné enamel. The art of enamelling is of great antiquity. It was fostered particularly in Byzantine workshops and at Limoges, so that many early pieces, like the famous Alfred jewel in the Ashmolean Museum in Oxford, were almost certainly importations mounted in this country. The Valence casket and the Warwick and Balfour of Burleigh ciboria are later examples.

The Studley bowl is a rare secular survival, and indicates the sumptousness of the last decades of the fourteenth century, when Richard II's interest in the arts created a court unequalled in taste and talent. But the story of secular patronage belongs to that era after 1485 when the Tudors succeeded the Plantagenets, and, more particularly, to the period after the Reformation.

Anglo Saxon brooch   Seventh century
Diam. 7.6 mm
This is one of a pair of brooches which were found on the breast of a skeleton at Milton North Field, near Abingdon in about 1832. The other is in the Ashmolean Museum at Oxford. It is made of gold and silver foil with enamel and garnet inlay, on a backing of copper and composition. The style of the brooch bears resemblance to pieces from the Sutton Hoo ship burial uncovered in 1939 and now in the British Museum. The latter included more than twenty pieces of gold jewellery set with several thousand cut garnets in a similar technique. On the evidence of coins found with these pieces they can be dated with some certainty to A.D. 625–30.

M.109–1939

Pectoral cross reliquary *c.* 1100 *H. 11.8 cm W. 4.4 cm D. 2.6 cm*
The box is made of walrus ivory, carved and pierced in low relief with foliate scrolls, birds and monsters, an anchor probably representing Ishmael, son of Abraham and Hagar, the *Agnus Dei*, and the symbols of the Evangelists. Attention was first drawn to the cross in 1855 when it was exhibited by Nathaniel Gould at a meeting of the British Archaeological Association. Nothing further was heard of it (and in 1962 it was published as lost) until 1966, when it was sent to Sotheby's for auction by a Bournemouth antique dealer. The decoration of the cross with interlaces of biting beasts caught in coils of foliage and tendril, and small human forms enmeshed in scrolls bears close comparison with Canterbury manuscripts, and it is thought that it was probably carved in the same school. A.6–1966

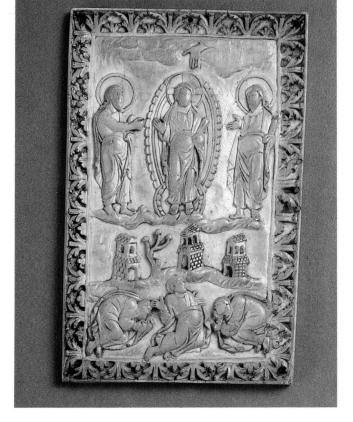

The Transfiguration Late tenth century *H. 14.2 cm W. 7.9 cm*
On the other side of this ivory plaque is a depiction of the Last Judgement. The plaque and a companion piece with a representation of the Ascension also in the Museum were catalogued for many years as Carolingian and related to the Rheims school of the ninth century. They are now thought, however, with a book cover in the Bibliothèque Nationale, Paris, to be copied from Rheims manuscripts in this country in the tenth and eleventh centuries. Such copying was considered quite acceptable at this time, the famous Utrecht Psalter being copied meticulously at Canterbury in about the year 1000.

253–1867

Head of a pastoral staff *c. 1180   H. 121 cm*
This crozier head, which is carved with scenes from the Life of Christ
and Life of St Nicholas, is one of the finest examples of English ivory
carving of the period. The original provenance of the crozier is not
clear, but one may assume that it was made either for the head of an
institution consecrated to St Nicholas or for an abbot or bishop of that
name. The carving is one of the exceedingly rare examples of the use of
elephant tusk in this country before the Gothic period.   218–1865

The Adoration of the Magi   Eleventh or twelfth century
H. 36 cm W. 16 cm
Various suggestions have been made as to the origin and dating of this
beautiful whalebone relief. Although usually accepted as English, some
authors have suggested that it may have been made in Ireland and
others that the style of carving relates most closely to that from
Northern France and Belgium. More recently it has been suggested
that the relief could be of Spanish origin. In general style the Adoration
shows a certain resemblance to some English manuscripts of the
twelfth century, and the awe-inspiring quality of the majestic figure of
the Virgin has been specifically likened to the great figures of the
stooping Christ on the rather earlier outline drawing of the Harrowing
of Hell in an English Psalter in the British Museum.   142–1866

The Gloucester candlestick Early twelfth century *H. 58.4 cm W. at base 20.3 cm*

First modelled in wax, then cast in bell-metal by the *cire-perdue* process, this candlestick is a splendid example of the technical skill of the craftsman in the early years of the twelfth century. The inscription round the stem tells that it was given by Peter, Abbot of Gloucester, to the church (now Cathedral) over which he ruled from 1104 to 1113. It is possible that the Gloucester Candlestick was looted from the church when it was destroyed by fire in 1122; a medieval inscription inside the grease-pan states that it was presented by one Thomas de Poche (perhaps not long after that date) to the Cathedral of Le Mans, where it remained until the French Revolution. It reappeared in the possession of an antiquary at Le Mans, who sold it to Prince Soltikoff, on the dispersal of whose collection in 1861, it was acquired by the Museum. 7649–1861

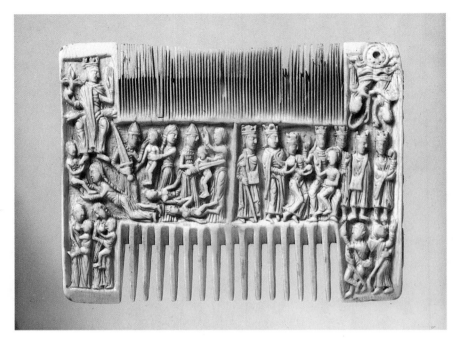

Liturgical comb *c.* 1120 *H. 7.5 cm W. 11.4 cm*
On one side the comb is carved with the Nativity, the Flight into Egypt, the Washing of the Feet of the Disciples, the last Supper, the Betrayal, the Crucifixion, and the Entombment; and on the other with the Massacre of the Innocents, the Adoration of the Magi, the Departure of the Magi, and the Annunciation to the Shepherds. The style of the carving compares closely with the historiated capital letters in the Psalter from St Albans, now at Hildesheim, which was completed before 1123. The comb of St Henry, now at Verdun, is also close in style and was probably produced in the same workshop.

A.27–1977

Leaf from a psalter *c.* 1130–50 ▷
H. 38 cm W. 26.7 cm
The forty-two pictures which cover both sides of the leaf illustrate the life of Christ from the Passion to Pentecost. It is one of four surviving leaves (the others are in the British Museum and in the Pierpoint Morgan Library, New York) which may have been part of the Eadwine Psalter, belonging to Trinity College, Cambridge, which was written at Canterbury in about 1147. 816–1894

The Warwick ciborium Late twelfth century *H. 120 cm Diam. 19.7 cm*
Copper gilt, engraved and enamelled, decorated with foliage enclosing figure subjects, representing various scenes from the Old Testament, including the Sacrifice of Cain and Abel, Moses and the burning bush, and Jonah issuing from the whale. The ciborium, which is missing its cover, was probably made in Winchester. There are no records of its whereabouts until 1717, when it was found in a brazier's shop in London. Later it entered the Warwick Castle Collection where it was burnt in the fire of 1871. It was probably as a result of this fire that much of the enamelling which originally decorated the ciborium was lost. Ciboria are receptacles used for the reservation of the Eucharist. M.159–1919

The Valence casket 1290–6   *H. 9.5 cm*
L. 17.8 cm W. 13.3 cm
The casket is made of copper engraved and
gilt, decorated in champlevé enamel with a
diaper of coats of arms representing William
de Valence, Earl of Pembroke (d.1296), and
some of his family connections, including the
royal house of England, the Dukes of Brit-
tany (Dreux), Angouleme, and Brabant, and
Lacy, Earl of Lincoln. The marriage of
Margaret of England with John, Duke of
Brabant which accounts for the presence of
his arms, took place in 1290. Four knobs are
missing from the lid. Caskets such as this
were probably used for the storage and safe
keeping of jewellery and other small precious
items.   4–1865

The Clare chasuble   *c.* 1275   ▷
L. 115.6 cm W. 66 cm
Silver-gilt and silver thread and coloured
silks in underside couching, split stitch and
laid and couched work on satin. The vestment has been severely cut down in the post-
medieval period. A stole and maniple with a
shield of arms at each end, which were
associated with the chasuble in 1786 but
have since disappeared, were perhaps made
of fragments from the original vestment; the
remains of a similar shield (probably arms of
Lacy) can be seen on the back of the
chasuble. The coats of arms suggest that the
work was commissioned by or for Margaret
Clare, wife of Edmund Plantagenet, Earl of
Cornwall, nephew to Henry III. Her marriage to the Earl, in 1272, remained child-
less, and she was divorced in 1294.   673–1864

Apparels of albs (detail)   1320–40   *H. 50.8 cm W. 81.3 cm*
The panel depicts the Nativity, the Annunciation, and the Three Kings, which are
embroidered on velvet with coloured silks and silver-gilt and silver thread in split stitch,
underside couching, laid and couched work, and raised work. The coats of arms are those of
Bardolf and another family. Like the Butler-Bowden Cope, this panel is typical of that phase
of *Opus Anglicanum* in which plain velvet grounds came into use, the embroidery being worked
on them through a piece of thin cloth on which the design was drawn and which was laid on
the pile surface to facilitate stitching.   8128–1863

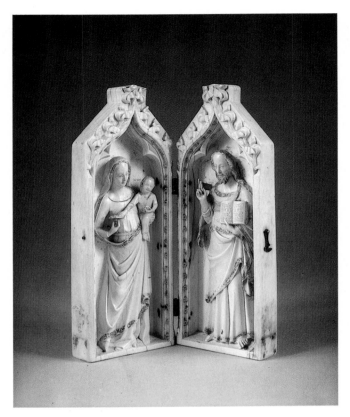

Diptych First half of the fourteenth century *H. 21.6 cm W. 16 cm*
The ivory Diptych is carved in deeply sunk relief, on the left wing with
the Virgin and Child, and on the right with Christ blessing. The hair,
the borders of the garments, and the rosettes on the inner margin are
gilded and there are very slight traces of colour. Although the group of
the Virgin and Child is composed on typical French lines, the massive
and monumental style which characterizes the carving is not found in
French work of this period. Other details, such as the long faces with
high rounded foreheads, seem peculiarly English in style. A.545-1910

Tile Early fourteenth century *L. 36 cm W. 20 cm*
The designs on this tile from Tring Church are taken from a
vernacular version of the Apocryphal Infancy Gospels describing the
miraculous childhood of Christ. The tile is an example of the so-
called *sgraffiato* technique, better known in pottery and fresco
decoration. Other tiles from the set are in the British Museum.
C.470-1927

The John of Thanet panel 1300–20 *H. 100 cm W. 41.5 cm*
Embroidered with silver-gilt and silver thread, coloured silks and
pearls, in underside couching and split stitch, on silk twill. The figure
of Christ is on a larger scale than any other example of English
medieval embroidery. He is depicted enthroned, holding the orb of the
world. Above the arch is the inscription JOHANNIS DE THANETO. John
Thanet was 'a Monk and Chaunter' of Canterbury Cathedral 'well-
vers'd in the Mathematicks; but especially skilled in Musick' who died
aged 92 in 1330. The panel was probably originally part of a Cope, and
the triangular void at the top of the design was originally covered by the
cope-hood. T.337-1921

The Ramsey Abbey censer   Second quarter of the fourteenth century   *H. 27.3 cm Diam. 14 cm*
This censer, the only example in silver-gilt of English workmanship of this date, was discovered in 1850 during the draining of Whittlesea Mere, Huntingdonshire. An incense boat and some pewter plates which were found with the censer include decoration in the form of a ram rising from the waves. This device is clearly a rebus for the name Ramsey and seems to indicate that the whole find was once the property of the neighbouring Abbey of Ramsey, unless it be supposed that the pieces bearing the rebus were gifts to the Abbey of Peterborough from the two abbots named Ramsey, who presided over it in the mid-fourteenth and late fifteenth century respectively.   M.268–1923

The Butler-Bowden cope (detail)
Second quarter of the fourteenth century
H. 162.8 cm W. 349 cm
Embroidered in silk, silver and silver-gilt
thread in underside-couching, split stitch,
and laid and couched work, on velvet; the
orphreys and hood of the cope, which are not
visible in this illustration, are of similar
materials and workmanship, on linen. The
cope was originally enriched with seed
pearls, of which only a few remain. Various
biblical scenes and saints and apostles are
depicted, of which this detail illustrates St
James the Great. The cope was cut up to
form another vestment but has now been
reassembled in its original form on a re-
placement velvet backing.   T.36–1955

The Syon cope   First quarter of the
fourteenth century   *H. 142 cm W. 292 cm*
Silk, silver, and silver-gilt thread in underside-couching, split stitch and laid and
couched work on linen; the orphreys and a
morse which is associated with the cope are
of similar materials in underside-couching,
cross and plait stitches. In the quatrefoils are
depicted various apostles and biblical subjects. The cope was originally made as a
chasuble, and fragments of quatrefoils containing four other Apostles which were muti-
lated during conversion, are to be seen at the
sides. The spaces between the quatrefoils
are occupied by angels, except for two
figures of a cleric bearing the inscription
DAVN: PERS: DE . . . [?], for whom, presumably, the vestment was made. The cope was
formerly in the possession of nuns from the
Bridgettine Foundation of Henry V at Syon,
Middlesex.   83–1864

The Studley bowl Late fourteenth
century *H. 14 cm Diam. 14.6 cm*
This covered bowl is the earliest piece of
English domestic silversmith's work in the
Museum. It was intended for porridge and
similar foods, and was for a time the property
of Studley Royal Church, near Ripon, Yorkshire. It is decorated with chased and engraved ornament, consisting, on each part, of
a black-letter alphabet preceded by a cross
and followed by various literal symbols and
contractions such as were used in contemporary Latin manuscripts, all springing from
a leafy wreath; on the knob of the cover is the
letter 'a'.   M.I–1914

Stained glass window *c.* 1400
H. 354 cm W. 165 cm
This stained glass window is made up
from three lights showing St John the
Evangelist, the Prophet Zephaniah, and
St James the Less. It formed part of the
original glazing of Winchester College
Chapel put in by order of the founder,
William of Wykeham, about 1400. Between 1822 and 1828 the old glass was
replaced by modern copies in the process
of 'restoration'. It closely resembles the
slightly earlier glass still in the Chapel of
William of Wykeham's other foundation
at New College, Oxford, and is remarkable for the fine detail of the painting and
the silvery effect of the white glass beside
panes of soft, rich colour. The work was
done by the glazier Thomas of Oxford,
using sheet glass imported from Northern France. The elaborate style of the
canopies is superior to that found in any
English glass of the later fifteenth century.   4237–1855

Enamelled gold rosary *c.* 1500   Largest
bead *L. 2.8 cm Diam. 1.9 cm*
The single rounded bead bears four panels
engraved with the Adoration of the Magi,
and the remaining beads are each engraved
with two figure subjects, with titles round
the edge in black letter. Two of the beads are
inscribed in a cursive script and are of a later
date. This is the earliest English rosary to
have survived. When first acquired by the
Museum it was assembled in a different,
apparently haphazard form so far as the
saints were concerned, and two of the large
beads were attached as a pendant. The
present arrangement corresponds with at
least one example of a rosary illustrated on a
medieval brass.   M.30–1934

The Swinburne pyx   *c.* 1320   *H. 2.8 cm*
Diam. 5.7 cm
A pyx is a small vessel, usually a round silver
box, in which the Sacrament is carried to the
sick. This example is made of parcel gilt and
was originally decorated with enamel, which
has since come off. The two subjects on the
cover of the pyx are copied from the arche-
type used for two manuscripts at Cambridge.
Interestingly, it is possible to connect genea-
logically the original owner of one of these
manuscripts, Alice de Reydon, *née* Reymes,
with ancestors of the Swinburnes of Pontop,
near Consett, to whom the pyx had belonged. The Museum purchased it from the
widow of the last remaining member of the
family.   M.15–1950

▽ **The Swansea altarpiece** Second half of the fifteenth century *H. 84 cm L. 213 cm* The altarpiece, which includes alabaster reliefs representing St John the Baptist, the Annunciation, the Nativity, the Holy Trinity, the Ascension, the Assumption, and St John in a framework of oak, was formerly in the collection of Lord Swansea at Singleton Abbey. Although a number of English alabaster altarpieces with the original wooden housing exist in France and Italy, this is the only one in Great Britain. The Museum has a large and comprehensive collection of English alabasters, many of which are on display. A.89–1919

Stained glass panels depicting cutting vines and harvesting corn First half of the fifteenth century *Diam. 20.3 cm*
These two panels are from a set of six in the Museum which depict the Labours of the Months. That showing a man cutting vines represents March and that depicting a man and woman reaping, August. Such subjects were popular for secular rather than church use at the time, and a number of sets are known, though most, like the Museum's, are incomplete. It has been suggested that the roundels may be Netherlandish, but the favour such series enjoyed in this country, the presence of one depicting Weeding (a subject which does not occur in contemporary continental manuscripts illustrating the months), and the character of the painting all point to an English origin. The roundels were formerly at Cassiobury Park, Hertfordshire. C.123–126–1923

Alabaster relief of the Tree of Jesse Early fifteenth century *H. 53.5 cm W. 28 cm*
Jesse is depicted on his right side, while from his breast the Tree or vine issues upward, the tendrils enclosing figures of Kings, maternal ancestors of Christ, and prophets who foretold his coming. In the centre of the upper part of the panel are the Virgin and Child enthroned. In the fourteenth and fifteenth centuries alabaster quarries were opened in Derbyshire, Staffordshire, and Nottinghamshire and centres of carving sprang up also in Lincoln and York. The material was much easier to carve than stone or wood and found a wide range of applications for ecclesiastical purposes. A.36–1954

Bust of Henry VII perhaps by Pietro Torrigiano (1472–1528)   First quarter of the sixteenth
century   *H. 91.4 cm W. 68.6 cm D. 35.6 cm*
The bust, which is made of painted and gilded terracotta, is life-size and shows the King late
in life. Its attribution to Torrigiano, which was first suggested in the eighteenth century, is
based not simply on comparison with that sculptor's known works, but also on the fact that the
bust bears a very strong resemblance to the figure on the bronze monument to Henry VII in
Westminster Abbey, which Torrigiano executed between 1511–17. The bust was formerly
associated with two others of Bishop Fisher and Henry VIII at Hatfield Peverell Priory, and
all three are said to have come from the Palace of Whitehall. It has also been conjectured that
they were commissioned by the Countess of Richmond, and that they were repaired by the
young John Flaxman in about 1769.   A.49–1935

Tudor (1485–1603)

Thomas Cromwell's fate, an earldom in April 1540 and a death sentence four months later, epitomizes the political and social uncertainty of Tudor England. New industries and fluctuating trade, coupled with outbursts of unrest at home and the successes and failures of an expansionist policy overseas, all led to a profound sense of instability. Yet the excitement, fragility, and tension which this created acted rather as a stimulant than a repressant to artists, writers, and craftsmen. It was, after all, the age which saw the supreme literary achievement of Shakespeare and the brilliant portraiture of Holbein and Hilliard.

Much of the story of Tudor decorative art has to do with the varying degrees by which it was influenced by classical canons of taste emanating from Italy and northern Europe. Interestingly, although Renaissance and other forms were freely adopted by craftsmen in this country, their work still retains an undeniably English quality. In architecture, for example, symmetry of plan and other classical concepts which were in common usage by the end of the century generally failed to impart a 'High Renaissance' quality. The effect of traditional elements asserted itself instead, even in houses such as Hardwick Hall, the design of which involved a great deal of classical thought.

The somewhat austere exterior of Hardwick, like that of many Tudor houses, contrasts strongly with the lavish interior with its elaborate plasterwork, panelling, painted decoration, and textile hangings. The design of these was based at first on naturalistic and geometric sources, such as had inspired medieval craftsmen, but these soon gave way to an increasing use of 'antique work'—the commoner Renaissance motifs—and strapwork and arabesque designs. The Museum's room from Sizergh Castle in Westmorland which was completed some time before 1582 reveals how widespread these designs became. The oak panelling is inlaid with arabesque patterns, now rather faded and discoloured with polish but clearly indicating their former splendour. The protruding porch is based on Flemish models and may be a little earlier in date.

In this and the adjoining gallery are displayed many examples of contemporary furniture: an oak bench dated 1562; an elmwood box with inlaid decoration in maple and other woods depicting flowers, birds, and figures resembling contemporary embroidery designs, which was probably used for storing small articles of clothing; a cupboard of typical form and decoration from the Moffat Collection; and a so-called 'Nonsuch' chest with elaborate inlay depicting buildings.

In the last of the Tudor galleries is that most famous of all beds, the Great Bed of Ware, and, next to it, examples of different tablewares including sets of beechwood roundels which were used as trenchers for the last course of a dinner, consisting of marzipan and other sweetmeats. A painted plaster frieze from Stodmarsh Court near Canterbury, with figures representing the planets after engravings by Virgil Solis of Nuremberg, dates from c. 1600 and serves as a reminder both of the importance of Continental source books and the popularity of bright painted decoration at this time. A rather false impression is conveyed by the present appearance of most movable furniture of this date. Although painting was unpopular in the fifteenth and early sixteenth centuries, it did undergo a revival after 1530 or so, and remained fashionable until upholstery in textiles became general at the close of the century.

Much Tudor plate was acquired as a means of storing wealth and was consequently sold in times of need. Since its value was assessed by weight, many pieces were melted down so as to be remade in more fashionable forms, and as a result much has disappeared. The Museum's mounted Cologne stoneware and oriental jugs, and the Howard Grace cup of 1525–6 have probably survived because they contain relatively little precious metal. Other pieces like the Richard Chester steeple cup of 1625–6, the Mostyn salt, or the less pretentious snuffers with the arms and initials of Edward VI have probably survived because of their intrinsic value.

One gallery is largely given over to textiles. Whereas most of those discussed in Chapter 1 were made for ecclesiastical use, after the Reformation weavers and embroiderers applied themselves instead to the elaboration of their clothes and homes. Walls were hung with tapestries or embroidered or painted hangings; beds were equipped with lavish sets of curtains and valances; tables and cupboards laid with cloths and carpets; and wooden chairs and benches covered with loose cushions. While some of these textiles were woven, most were embroidered. Indeed, during the Elizabethan period the work of amateurs assumed for the first time an equal importance with that of professionals.

Most of the formal court costumes lavishly embroidered with metal thread and jewels have now vanished. Some idea of their splendour can be gained from the Museum's superb collection of contemporary miniatures by Hans Holbein, Nicholas Hilliard, and Isaac Oliver. To these has recently been added Rowland Lockey's miniature of Thomas More and his family of c. 1600. What is so appealing about these miniatures is not just their refreshing naturalism, but their insistence on individual character as reflected by external appearance. They foreshadow the greater freedom both of expression and emotional content which typifies not just miniature painting but all the arts during the next era.

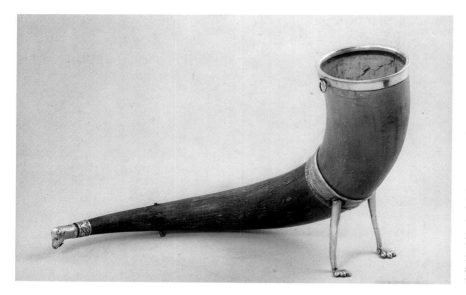

The Pusey horn Mid fifteenth century
H. 25.4 cm W. 44.5 cm
Only five medieval drinking horns are known to have survived. Unlike earlier examples they are equipped with feet so that they could be set down, and the small end of the horn is finished with a head, sometimes that of a man or, as in this example, of a monster. The Museum's horn, which was mounted in the fifteenth century, is said to have been given by King Canut to William Pusey, together with the Manor of that name, as a reward for having saved him from a surprise attack by the Saxons, and an inscription on the silver band testifies to this. M.220–1938

Monument to Sir Thomas Moyle (d. 1560) **and his wife Katherine** (d. after 1560)   About 1560   *H. 115.6 cm L. 217.2 cm W. 116.8 cm*
This monument is one of the most important of several acquired by the Museum from the ruined church of St Mary, Eastwell, Kent. Sir Thomas Moyle was the grandfather of Sir Moyle Finch and great-grandfather of Sir Heneage Finch. It was to Sir Heneage that Queen Elizabeth I is recorded to have presented the Armada Jewel (see p. 35). The stone of which the monument is constructed must have been formerly used in a building, since inside the tomb-chest are quatrefoil decoration, arch mouldings, and part of a window-transom. The church of St Mary at Eastwell had badly deteriorated by the end of the War, and in 1951 a gale blew down part of the nave roof. Every effort was made to find a home for the monuments, but without success, and during 1967–8 they were brought up to London and installed in the Museum.

A.187–1969

Close helmet *c. 1540   H. 25.4 cm W. 28 cm*

This helmet was acquired by the Museum as part of a composite half-armour of mainly German provenance. The profile of the helmet is, however, unmistakably that of the Royal armourers' workshops established by Henry VIII within the precincts of the Royal Palace at Greenwich. The visor resembles in form that in the Genouilhac armour of 1527 in the Metropolitan Museum of Art, New York, but the slightly higher comb indicates a later date. There is a Greenwich helmet of similar form in Croydon Parish Church.   M.504–1927

Table desk *c. 1525   H. 25 cm W. 40.6 cm D. 29 cm*

This highly ornate and important table desk, covered with painted and gilt leather, bears the heraldic badges of Henry VIII and Katherine of Aragon—the Portcullis, the Tudor Rose, the impaled Rose and Pomegranate, the Fleur-de-lis, the Castle (with cypher H. R.), and the Sheaf of Arrows. On the inner lid are painted the Royal Arms encircled by the garter, with boys blowing trumpets as supporters. On either side, standing beneath canopies, are figures of Mars in armour and Venus with Cupid, the design being executed with great spirit after woodcuts (*c.* 1510) by Hans Burgkmair, the celebrated German engraver. Such desks were introduced into England in the early Tudor period and used for the storage of scissors, penknives, and other small items.   W.29–1932

The Mostyn salt 1586–7. *H. 47 cm*
D. 18.4 cm
This is the most notable of the small group
of pieces of Elizabethan plate which the
Museum acquired from the ancient Welsh
family of Mostyn in 1886. From the Middle
Ages to the 1650s the great salt marked the
place of the host at the dining table, and the
present piece is a very fine example of one of
the standard designs of the second half of the
sixteenth century. The cylindrical body is
richly embossed with strapwork, cartouches,
masks, fruit, etc., whilst the cover is sur-
mounted by a vase, which must have originally contained flowers. It bears the Goldsmith's mark 'T' in a pearled border and a
London hallmark for 1586–7.   146–1886

Glass attributed to Giacomo
Verzelini 1581 *H. 20.6 cm*
Giacomo Verzelini was the leader of a party
of nine Italian glass makers who settled in a
glass house in Crutched Friars in London in
1571. Born in Venice, Verzelini acquired the
royal privilege as sole producer of 'Venice
Glasses' in 1575, and kept it until his
retirement twenty-one years later. During
this time he not only established himself as
the foremost glass manufacturer in the country, but also established a rather less elaborate form of Venetian design which was to
dominate English glass design for the next
one hundred years.   C.523–1936

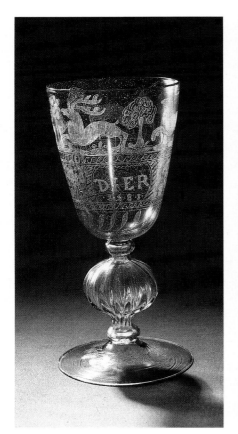

The Bradford table carpet (detail)   Late sixteenth century   *L. 396 cm W. 175 cm.*
Embroidery on linen canvas in tent stitch or varieties of cross stitch first came into
prominence during the Elizabethan period and was much used for furnishing purposes. The
subject-matter often reflected the Elizabethan's delight in gardens and the countryside, and
motifs abstracted from these sources were frequently made into patterns of a formal type,
such as the exuberant vine twined around a trellis in this table carpet. Typical country views
with shepherds, hunting scenes, and anglers, such as form a border to the carpet, were also

Miniature portrait of Margaret Pemberton by Hans Holbein
(1497?–1543)   *c.* 1536   *Diam. 5.2 cm*
The sitter can be identified by the coat of arms of her husband
Robert Pemberton, which is painted on vellum on the back. The
inscription in gold on the background indicates that she was twenty-
three years old when the portrait was painted. Barely a dozen
miniatures are now accepted as being by Holbein and it is generally
agreed that this is the finest.   P.40–1935

Miniature portrait of Queen Elizabeth I by Nicholas Hilliard
(1547–1619)   *c.* 1588   *H. 4.4 cm*
This is the earliest portrait of Elizabeth I in the collection and
belongs to a group of miniatures and large-scale portraits which all
seem to derive from the same face-mask. In the Queen's hair is a
crescent-moon-shaped jewel, the earliest allusion in miniatures to
the cult of Elizabeth as the moon goddess, Diana or Cynthia, which
was to become the dominant reference in miniatures at the close of
the reign. The mount appears to be late seventeenth century.   P.23–1975

popular. Like oriental rugs, many embroidered carpets were considered too precious to risk damage on the floor at this time and were placed over tables instead. This carpet came from the collection of the Earl of Bradford.

T.134–1928

The Danny jewel Second half sixteenth century *L. (with chains) 8.9 cm W. 6 cm*
The jewel is in the form of a pendant and is made from a half section of a narwhal's tusk mounted in enamelled gold. At the top is a cavity which was probably intended for a charm. Narwhal's tusk, or 'unicorn's horn' as it was sometimes referred to, was itself considered a protection against bad luck and poisoning. A pendant pearl probably hung originally from the bottom. The jewel was formerly the property of the Campions of Danny, Sussex. A similar jewel is depicted in Zucchero's portrait of Robert Bristowe, purse-bearer to Queen Elizabeth I; and another made of 'golde' set with 'unicornes horne' is referred to in the will of Edward Lyttelton of Longford, Salop. M.97–1917

The Armada jewel *c.* 1600 *H. 7 cm*
Enamelled gold set with diamonds and rubies. Under a convex glass on the front is a high-relief profile bust of Queen Elizabeth I, and the back forms a locket enclosing a miniature painting of the Queen dated 1580 by Nicholas Hilliard. This masterpiece of fine casting, the beauty of which is enhanced by its background of blue translucent enamel, appears to have been a gift of the Queen to Sir Thomas Heneage in reward of his services as Treasurer-at-War at the time of the Armada. M.81–1935

Miniature portrait of a lady called Frances, Countess of Somerset (1590–1632) by Isaac Oliver (d. 1617)   *Diam. 13 cm*
Isaac Oliver was born in France but was brought to England while still a child, and in 1606 became a British citizen. He received his early training under Nicholas Hilliard, but amplified this with visits to the Low Countries and to Venice. This miniature is typical of Oliver's best work, in which he combines the ambitious ideas of scale and complexity which he picked up on the Continent, with the tradition of the portrait miniature he learned from Hilliard. It was formerly in the possession of Horace Walpole, who inscribed a paper label on the back of the frame with the name of the sitter.   P.12–1971

Bag and pincushion   First quarter seventeenth century   ▷
Bag 14 × 11.4 cm Pincushion 6.4 × 5.4 cm
Linen canvas embroidered with silver thread and silk in tent and plaited Gobelin stitches, lined with green silk. Embroidery was a popular art in the sixteenth and seventeenth centuries, many of the patterns deriving from illuminated manuscripts, particularly that involving coiled tendrils infilled with flowers, birds, animals, and insects which appears on many examples of Elizabethan costume in the Museum's collection. Bags with attached pincushions such as this were hung at the waist.   316–1898

The Barbor jewel Second half sixteenth century *L. 6 cm W. 3.2 cm*
The jewel is made of enamelled gold, set with rubies and diamonds enclosing an onyx cameo of Queen Elizabeth I; and hung with a cluster of pearls. On the back is an enamelled oak tree. According to Fox's *Book of Martyrs*, William Barbor of London (d. 1586) 'for his firm adherence to the Protestant Religion was to suffer at the Stake . . . News came the Queen was dead, so that Popish party did not dare to put him to Death. In Remembrance of so Eminent a preservation . . . [he] had the effigies of Queen Elizabeth cut out upon stone; bequeathing the jewel to his elder Son, if he had a daughter and names her Elizabeth'.
889–1894

An unknown youth leaning against a tree by Nicholas Hilliard (1546–1619) *c.* 1588 *H. 13.4 cm W. 7 cm*
In this full-length portrait, the love-sick pose and the symbolisms of the thorn-bearing rose-tree are underlined by the Latin inscription at the top of the miniature, *Dat poenas laudata fides* ('My praised faith causes my sufferings'). The identity of the sitter and the cause of his melancholy are not recorded, but since Hilliard was a favourite of Elizabeth, it may depict a member of her intimate circle.
P.163–1910

Clock 1588 *H. 33 cm W. 16.7 cm*
This is the earliest known dated English clock. The case is of gilt brass and is inscribed 'Frauncoy Nowe fecit a London A°Din°
1588'. The engraved decoration is probably based on designs by Etienne de Laune and Abraham de Bruyn and is very similar to
that on the Magdalen Cup in the Manchester City Art Gallery, which bears the London Hallmark for 1573–4. The astronomical
dials which are shown separately indicate the date, the astrological indication, the phases and age of the moon, and the times of
high tide at London Bridge. The thirty hour, three chain movement, the hour and quarter bells, and the twenty-four hour
chapter ring are all of late seventeenth century date. Although Francis Nowe set up his workshops in London, he was born in
Brabant.
M.39–1959

38

The Vyvyan salt 1592–3 *H. 34 cm*
D. 40 cm
The Vyvyan Salt, so named from its having
been for over 250 years in the possession of
the Vyvyans of Trelowarren, Cornwall, is
among the most important pieces of English
sixteenth-century silversmiths' work in existence. The great attraction of the Salt lies in
the panels and small medallions of *verre
églomisé* (glass decorated at the back with foil
and colours) based on designs in Geoffrey
Whitney's *Choice of Emblems*, published in
1586; the medallions bear heads of Ninus,
Cyrus, Alexander, and Julius Caesar. It was
made by a goldsmith who used a mark
consisting of the letters WH and a flower,
the London Hallmark for 1592–3 is re-
peated on the body, the foot, and the
cover.   M.273–1925

The Great Bed of Ware About 1580 *H. 266 cm W. 326 cm D. 337 cm*

Carved oak with painted and inlaid decoration. There is probably no more famous piece of English furniture than the Great Bed of Ware. It seems likely that it was made for the White Hart Inn at Ware where it is first recorded in 1610. The earliest reference to the bed occurs in Shakespeare's *Twelfth Night*, which was first performed in 1601, and it is mentioned by numerous travellers, historians, playwrights, poets (including Byron), antiquarians, and gossips, right through into the nineteenth century. The bed is just over ten feet square, but its size quickly came to be greatly exaggerated, one writer claiming in 1736 that '26 butchers and their wives' had slept in it.   w.47–1931

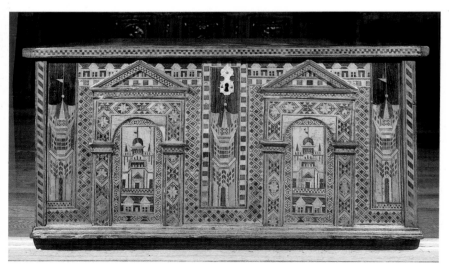

Coffer Late sixteenth century
H. 58.4 cm W. 123 cm D. 58.4 cm
Oak with marquetry of bog and cherry-wood. The name 'Nonsuch' or 'Nonesuch' is often given to early inlaid chests of this type, in which the design of the inlay is architectural in character and represents a quaint building with castellations, high-pitched roofs, cupolas and steeples set with vanes, and flying flags. It probably derives from Nonsuch or Nonesuch Palace, which was built by Henry VIII at Ewell in Surrey, and so-called as being without equal, although it has also been suggested that the term may derive from Nonsuch House on London Bridge. In point of fact there is no reason to suppose that either of these buildings is represented rather than any other typical Tudor or Elizabethan House.   342–1905

The Oxburgh hangings (detail)   *c.* 1570   *H. 84 cm W. 91 cm*
The Museum was very fortunate to acquire in 1955 thirty-nine panels embroidered by Mary, Queen of Scots and Elizabeth, Countess of Shrewsbury. This detail of the central panel of a hanging depicts feathers falling around an armillary sphere and is inscribed with a motto which translated means 'Sorrows pass but hope abides'. In the border are the arms of England, Scotland, France, and Spain and emblems copied from Claude Paradin *Devises Heroïques*, Lyon, 1557. The embroidery is in coloured silks and silver-gilt thread in cross, tent and long-armed cross stitches on canvas and is applied to green velvet.   T·33–1955

The Bostocke sampler 1598 *W. 35.6 cm L. 42.5 cm*
This sampler of linen embroidered in coloured silks, metal
thread, seed pearls, and black beads is the earliest dated
sampler so far recorded. It is called after Jane Bostocke, the
embroideress whose name appears one-third of the way down
with the alphabet. The stitches used include back, Algerian
eye, satin, arrowhead, chain, ladder, button hole, and de-
tached button-hole fillings, couching in patterns, coral, speck-
ling, two-sided Italian cross, bullion, and French knots and
beadwork. It is possible that three small animals were
unpicked, or that the stitching has simply worn away. The
Museum's collection of textiles includes numerous samplers,
many of which can be seen in the Textile Study Rooms.

T.190–1960

Panel from a tapestry map by William Sheldon *c.* 1588
L. 126.4 cm W. 65.4 cm
This panel and another also in the Museum originally formed
part of the lower right-hand corner of a map of Oxfordshire
and Berkshire. Both pieces were formerly in the collection of
Horace Walpole and are recorded in the Strawberry Hill Sale
catalogue of 1842. There the figures depicted in the border of
this panel are described as Anthony and Cleopatra, but it is,
perhaps, more likely that they represent Temperance with
either Perseus or Mercury. William Sheldon was the first
person to establish Tapestry weaving on a commercial basis in
this country. A country gentleman of the Midlands who made
a fortune in the wool trade, he expressly stated in his will that
his aim was to provide work for the unemployed and to keep in
the country money that would otherwise be spent in buying
tapestries abroad.

T.61–1954

Tapestry cushion-cover *c.* 1600
H. 45.7 cm W. 48.3 cm
This charming and simple cushion-cover, which depicts the Flight into Egypt, was also made in William Sheldon's workshop. The purity of colour and fine technique and sympathetic treatment of the animals and flowers are characteristic of the art of the period. William Sheldon's weavers under Richard Huckes, who died in 1621 aged 97, and his son Francis produced many magnificent works, and it must have been particularly upsetting for them when the official order for a set of tapestries to commemorate the Armada went to Holland. The workshops, which closed down in 1647, were situated at Barcheston in Warwickshire in a farm building which still survives. Another similar cushion-cover is also in the Museum's collection (T.85–1913).   T.191–1926

Gamecock salt   *c.* 1570–80   *H. 26.7 cm L. 14 cm W. 8.3 cm*
The salt is made from a Nautilus shell mounted in silver gilt. The head unscrews to form a caster and the lower part of the neck acts as a container, presumably for spices. The salt was held in a silver gilt container fitted into the shell. *Nautilus pompilus* was first caught for food, but by the sixteenth century the Chinese had begun to carve the shell. During the early seventeenth century, Amboyna, where many nautilus were caught, had become one of the trading posts of the Dutch East India Company, and shells were brought back to Europe. They were still considered very rare and precious, however, and were frequently mounted in gold and silver. The Museum's example bears no hallmarks but is typical Elizabethan work of the period 1570–80.   M.13–1969

Earthenware dish depicting the Fall   1635   *Diam. 48.3 cm*

The last part of the fifteenth century and the early sixteenth century saw the rise in Italy of the manufacture of tin-enamelled pottery painted in bright colours, which is called maiolica. The pottery quickly spread throughout Europe and acquired distinct national schools of decoration. In the North the Netherlandish cities of Antwerp and Delft became the centres of manufacture specializing particularly in blue-and-white wares, and it was from there that the craft moved to England. The first centres of manufacture here were on the Thames at Lambeth, Southwark, and Bermondsey. The earliest dated piece is a dish of 1601 in the London Museum. This is very much in the Dutch style, whereas the Museum's dish, which is dated 1635, is similar to another in the British Museum and represents a less-accomplished and characteristically English version of this style. Such big dishes, archaistically named 'chargers', were used primarily to decorate sideboards or chimney pieces. Later their manufacture also spread to Bristol and Liverpool. Many were decorated with blue stripes around their rims in imitation of Delft plates, hence the description 'blue dash chargers'.

C.26–1931

Jacobean (1603–1715)

Just as the arts of the Elizabethan age had been marked by a growing awareness of the Italian and northern European Renaissance, so the dominant theme of the Jacobean period was the influence upon it of other cultures. Initially, however, there was little indication of impending change. James I, Jacobus, after whom the era is named, did bring with him a Scottish court, but this had little impact on the simple, essentially domestic community of the Tudor age. Solid, useful pieces of furniture such as long tables, press cupboards, and settles; silver influenced by German sheets of designs; lead glazed earthenware; and tent-stitch embroidery on canvas continued to be popular.

By the second quarter of the century, increasing wealth from foreign trade began to show itself, particularly by the large number of houses which were either rebuilt or remodelled. These, following the example set by Inigo Jones at Queen's House, had more and smaller rooms than their Tudor counterparts, and consequently required different furnishings. For example, although some large pieces of plate continued to be made for decorative purposes, the great salt and elaborate cups gave way to smaller, more personal items, and silver became more popular than gold. Similarly, in ceramics the large tin glazed earthenware or Delftware dishes were intended for display, whilst smaller pieces were made for daily use.

Stylistically the arts of the Low Countries and of France became more influential at this time, stimulated not just by Charles I's marriage to Henrietta Maria of France, but also by his encouragement of Rubens, Van Dyck, and many other distinguished foreign artists who came to work in Britain. Charles also acquired many important works of art from abroad, the best known of which are undoubtedly the famous cartoons by Raphael depicting the Acts of the Apostles, now on loan to the Museum from Her Majesty The Queen. The influence of the cartoons, as the design of the interior of Ham House indicates, was considerable.

Foreign influence was further encouraged after the Restoration in 1660. Charles II and his supporters had spent much of their exile in France and Holland, and as a consequence their taste had shifted away from the Italianism of Inigo Jones. Hugh May's 'Dutch' Eltham Lodge, and William Talman's Chatsworth, influenced by Versailles, both set new architectural standards, out of which the great Baroque buildings such as Castle Howard and Blenheim by Vanbrugh and his contemporaries later evolved. At the same time Wren was introducing Baroque features derived from Continental sources in his London churches, the rebuilding of many of which was made necessary by the Great Fire of 1666.

In the applied arts these sympathies were reflected not just by changes of style and form, but also by the introduction of new materials and techniques. For example, walnut was first extensively used for furniture during the reign of Charles II, when veneering was introduced and caning and gilding were practised for the first time. The naturalistic designs found in marquetry cabinets and other pieces of furniture, like the carvings of Grinling Gibbons, reflect the influence of contemporary Dutch still life painting. One important new piece of furniture introduced at this time is illustrated by the bookcase with glazed doors, which is seen to be very similar to those in the Pepys Library at Magdalene College, Cambridge.

A silver dressing-table set chased with scenes copied from Chinese prints serves as a reminder that the Dutch East India Company was responsible for introducing many Oriental objects to the West. Porcelain was particularly popular. Some pieces had reached this country in the sixteenth century, but it was not until after 1618 that they were imported in any quantity. Some large pieces were mounted in silver for decorative purposes in continuance of the earlier tradition, but many smaller wares, particularly bowls and dishes, were used especially for the drinking of tea. Like coffee 'black as soote, and tasting not much unlike it', as one contemporary writer remarked, tea seems to have been introduced here during the Restoration. The fine earthenwares of Dwight and the Elers Brothers based on these Oriental pieces represent the first serious attempts to imitate porcelain in this country. Another facet of Oriental influence was the vogue for lacquered screens and panels, frequently mounted as doors and fronts to cabinets, which resulted in the establishment of an English school of lacquering. Several japanned cabinets mounted on elaborate carved and sometimes silvered stands are shown in the Primary Galleries.

The dominant theme of the closing decades of the Stuart era was the influence of the large influx of Huguenot craftsmen who settled in this country. Not only were many industries revitalized as a result, like that of silk weaving at Spitalfields, but Huguenot styles gradually replaced the Dutch designs and were consequently largely responsible for the appearance of what is now called the 'Queen Anne Style'. Most influential of the designers was probably Daniel Marot, who followed William of Orange to this country in 1694 and was employed by the King at Hampton Court. His sheets of printed designs published in 1702 and 1712 were widely copied and adapted by British craftsmen. Other Huguenot craftsmen, like the silversmiths Paul Platel, and Paul de Lamerie, who settled in London with his parents in 1691, introduced radically new forms based to a large extent on the earlier ornament of Du Cerceau, Jean Berain, and Jean le Pautre, which were to prove particularly influential in the Georgian era.

The Betley window (detail)   *c. 1621   H. 67.3 cm W. 39.4 cm*
This panel of painted glass depicting Morris dancers and figures from the Robin Hood games celebrating a 'Mery May' derives its name from Betley Old Hall in Staffordshire, where it first came to light in a room bearing the date 1621. Although the figures of the six dancers, one of which is illustrated here, and the musician are based on a print by Israhel Van Meckenham of about 1460–70, the clothes they wear are typical of a period some 30 or 40 years later. But enamel colours in which the pictures are painted were not in use until the mid sixteenth century, and it is likely that the panel was executed in about 1621, the date when Betley Old Hall seems to have been built.   C.248–1976

The Calverley toilet service   1683–4   *Mirror H. 57.2 cm W. 37.5 cm*
Although Renaissance inventories show that ladies already possessed a number of silver toilet utensils, the manufacture of whole sets does not seem to have begun before the Restoration. When such services ceased to be appreciated, they were generally broken up and dispersed so that there are now very few surviving sets which are nearly complete. The Museum's set, which was once the property of the Calverley family of Yorkshire, includes only a dozen pieces, whereas a set in the Farrer Collection includes twenty-eight pieces.   240–to 240m–1879

Mermaid ewer and basin   1610–11.   *Ewer H. 31.1 cm L. 21 cm. Basin H. 43.8 cm W. 45.3 cm D. 9.5 cm*
The ewer and basin had no provenance until 1928, when it was illustrated in a short article in *Old Furniture*. Escutcheons on the chest of the mermaid and in the centre of the scallop-shaped basin are engraved with the armorials of Sir Thomas Wilson (*c.* 1560–1619), author and Italian scholar, who was a protegé of the Cecils, and prosecutor of Sir Walter Raleigh. Ewers and basins were used by diners to wash their hands before a meal. Although originally introduced before the popularization of forks made eating with the fingers unnecessary, they continued to be made until the early eighteenth century.   M.10 and a–1974

Watch *c.* 1640–50 *H. 11.7 cm W. 9.3 cm*
This watch was made by Edward East, who held the appointment of
watchmaker to Charles I and has been described as the most famous
maker of his time. He was one of the original assistants of the
Clockmaker's Company, named in its Charter of Incorporation in
1632, and became Master of the Company in 1645 and again in
1652. The existence of a number of watches bearing the name
'Edwardus East Londini', or similar, which are stylistically of dates in
the third quarter of the century, has led to the supposition that there
may have been a father and son of the same name.   M.64–1952

Tapestry depicting Hero and Leander   First half of the
seventeenth century   *H. 426.7 cm L. 548.6 cm*
Hero is represented mourning over the dead body of Leander. This
tapestry is one of a set of six representing the history of Hero and
Leander which were made at the tapestry workshops inaugurated at
Mortlake by James I in 1619. The cartoons for the series were
designed by Francis Clein, a native of Mecklenburg and former
court-painter of Christian IV of Denmark, who was artistic director
of the factory until his death in 1658. In the bottom right hand corner
is the mark of Sir Francis Crane, who was appointed first Director of
the factory and remained so until 1636. The factory was closed
down in 1703. Other Mortlake sets of Hero and Leander woven
after the same designs are in the Swedish Royal Collection at
Stockholm and at Hardwick Hall.   T.370–1910

Carpet (detail) 1672   *H. 348 cm × 233.7 cm*
The Museum possesses two remarkable English seventeenth-century carpets, both of which bear dates. The earlier (710–1904) is inscribed 'Feare God and Keepe His Commandements Made in the Yeare 1603', and the later, of which this is a detail, bears a shield containing the arms of Molyneux and Rigby and the date 1672. Both are made with woollen piles and Turkish knots. Although attempts were made to introduce the craft of carpet-knotting into this country at least as early as 1579, when it was proposed to bring over some Persian carpet weavers, the commercial production of carpets did not get under way here until the eighteenth century. Previously, knotted textiles, sometime called turkey work, tended to be made on a small scale for chair backs and seats, etc., rather than as carpets.   T.132–1924

Embroidered miniature of Charles I *c. 1640–50* *H. 10.2 cm*
W. 11 cm
A number of small needlework portraits of Charles I such as this are
known. They show skill of such a high order that it has been
suggested that they are not the work of amateurs but of one particular
atelier, and that they were probably made as gifts for the King himself
or his friends, or for persons who wished to have memorial portraits
of the King after his execution. They fall into two or three groups,
and are copied from portraits by Van Dyck or his imitators.   812–1891

Charles I by Hubert Le Sueur (1595?–1650) 1631
H. 87.6 cm
Hubert Le Sueur was born in France but came to England
sometime before 1626. A considerable number of busts of
Charles I have been attributed to him, but the Museum's bust
is the earliest signed and dated example recorded. It is very
close in style and modelling to a number of bronzes, and since
Le Sueur was better known for his work in that medium it has
been suggested that this marble bust may have been a copy by
some carver employed in his workshop. The rather stiff
posture of the sitter and richly fashioned armour are characteristic of Le Sueur, whose most famous work is the bronze
equestrian statue of Charles I at Charing Cross.   A.35–1910.

Goblet by George Ravenscroft (1618–81)
H. 16.5 cm
George Ravenscroft, a shipowner, merchant, and amateur chemist, was employed by the London Glass Company in 1673 to produce a substitute for Venetian crystal glass from materials available in this country. After a series of experiments mainly designed to remove 'crisseling', he discovered in 1675 that the addition of lead oxide provided a fine-quality clean glass. Ravenscroft's experiments and glass were made in glasshouses he built on or near the site of the Savoy and at Henley-on-Thames.   C.530–1936

The Moody salt   1664   *H. 19 cm*
W. 19.7 cm
Although known as the Moody salt and pricked with the initials AVM, it was not originally made for that family but came into their possession in about 1730 through Ursula Sadleir, the last representative of the Sadleirs of Apsley Guise. The salt is made of silver, chased and repoussé, and bears a London hallmark. Stylistically it is typical of the simpler types of salt which were popular for some fifty years or so after the death of Charles I. Most were circular, square, or octagonal, with a waist and cavity on top. The scrolled brackets which form perhaps the most characteristic feature of the group were to support a dish of fruit, as is clearly seen in many Dutch pictures.   M.347–1912

Panelled room from Clifford's Inn   1686–8
This room of oak panelling with applied carvings in cedar is an
excellent example of the way in which the pure Palladian classicism of
Inigo Jones was domesticated by English architects of the late
seventeenth century. Above the overmantle is a shield bearing the
arms of Penhallow quartering Penwarin, which refer to the marriage
in the reign of Henry VII of John Penhallow with Mary, daughter and
co-heiress of Vivian Penwarin. The room was reconstructed for their
descendant John Penhallow, who in 1674 was admitted to the Society
of Clifford's Inn, an organization which leased rooms in their
property, originally an Inn of Chancery, to suitable tenants. After the
rebuilding of the original Court in 1686, John Penhallow had his new
rooms redecorated, and he moved into them in 1688.   1029–1903

Lime wood cravat   Late seventeenth century   *H. 24 cm W. 21 cm*
This remarkable lime wood cravat, carved by Grinling Gibbons
(1648–1721) in imitation Venetian point lace, was formerly in the
possession of Horace Walpole and hung in his house at Strawberry
Hill. On 11 May 1769, Walpole described to George Montague how
at a frolic of several days before he had received a number of
distinguished foreign guests wearing the cravat and a pair of James I's
embroidered gloves, and how 'the French servants stared and firmly
believed that this was the dress of an English country gentleman.'
When Walpole's collection was dispersed in 1842 the cravat was
purchased by Miss (Baroness) Burdett-Coutts and remained in her
house in London until her death in 1906.   w.181–1928

Abigail Pett bedhangings (detail)   Late seventeenth century
The Tudor and early Stuart vogue for tent stitch cushion-covers, bed valances, and table-carpets worked in crewels (i.e. worsteds) was succeeded, probably at some date in the reign of Charles I, by that for sets of bed-curtains, embroidered mainly in the new long and short stitch, with details in stem and other stitches, and French knots. The ground material is uniformly a twill, with linen warp and cotton weft, the average loom-width being nineteen inches. The set consisted of two wide curtains at the foot of the bed made from five breadths, two on either side made from two-and-a-half or three breadths; three narrow valances, and three 'bases'. Most sets are anonymous, but this particular one bears an embroidered inscription indicating that it was made by Abigail Pett, an amateur embroideress.   T.13–1929

Upholstered chair   *c.* 1660   *H. 94 cm*
W. 52 cm D. 50.8 cm
The chair is made of turned walnut with upholstered back and seat covered in tent stitch embroidery on a linen canvas ground. The embroidery, which displays the arms of Hill of Spaxton Yarde and Poundsford, Somerset, impaling Gurdon of Assington Hall, Suffolk, and Letton of Norfolk, dates from 1641–55. That the chair is of a slightly later date than this is indicated by the barley sugar turning of the legs. The coloured crewel fringe is original. This type of chair appears very frequently in illustrations of interiors between the late sixteenth century and about 1670. Surprisingly, however, comparatively few now survive. The reason for this lies in the fact that the chairs were so simple, and it was found easier to discard them once their textile covers became worn rather than to have them re-upholstered. The turning and elaborate embroidery on the present example probably account for its having been preserved. Chairs such as this are commonly called 'farthingale chairs', or in seventeenth century inventories 'chaises à demoiselle', because they were most frequently used by women who found them convenient when wearing voluminous skirts held out by padded farthingales.   W.124–1937

'Lord and Lady Clapham' 1695–1700 *H. 54.6 cm*
These painted wooden dolls dressed in contemporary clothes of
the late seventeenth century are the largest and earliest fully-
dressed dolls known. The delicately painted eyes and eyebrows,
scarlet lips, and well-rouged cheeks are in a remarkable state of
preservation. The dolls were known in the previous owner's
family as Lord and Lady Clapham since their ancestors owned
property there. Particularly noteworthy among the dolls ac-
cessories are her very rare black silk mask with glass bead in the
mouth, and his hat, which bears the trade label of 'T. Bourdillon.
Hosier and Hatter to his Majesty'. The armchairs in caned
beechwood and elmwood are contemporary with the dolls.
T.846 and 847–1974

Fulham stoneware figure of Lydia Dwight *c.* 1674
H. 28.6 cm
This figure of a little girl represents Lydia Dwight, who died on 3
March 1674. Born in 1667, she was the daughter of John Dwight,
a notary public of the Restoration period and a man of scientific
interests who devoted himself, amongst other things, to experiments in making new kinds of pottery. Imitating and refining the
German types of stoneware, he sought also to discover the secret
of Chinese porcelain. To facilitate his experiments, Dwight set up
a pottery which still exists at Fulham, where he produced not only
useful wares but also a number of beautiful busts and statuettes
anticipating in a remarkable manner eighteenth-century porcelain
figures.
1054–1871

Boy playing the bagpipes by Caius Gabriel Cibber (1630–1700)   *c.* 1680–90.
H. 112 cm

This Portland stone group was probably made for Archibald, First Duke of Argyll. It was at Whitton Park, the 3rd Duke's home before coming to London, where it was first in Long Acre and then in Tottenham Court Road until 1835. Later still it figured in the Stowe sale of 1848 and was subsequently at Snitterfield, Warwickshire and Welcombe, Stratford-on-Avon. The group has been associated with Defoe's 'Blind Piper', whose experiences in the plague cart are described in the *Journal of the Plague,* but there are, it seems, no grounds for this. Cibber was born in Denmark and worked in Italy before coming to England. His best-known works in this country are probably the monument to Thomas Sackville (d. 1677) at Withyam in Sussex, and 'Melancholy' and 'Raving Madness', the two figures, recently aquired by the Museum, which he carved for the portico of Bethlem Hospital in *c.* 1680. Although Cibber married Jane Colley, the daughter of William Colley of Glaston, Rutland, who brought him a dowry of £6,000, he was, nevertheless, always in financial difficulties. Indeed, he was arrested for debt and confined in the King's Bench at the time he was cutting reliefs on the Monument in London (1673–5), but was allowed out from the prison to continue his work and forced to return there every night.   A.3–1930

Stoneware teapot   Late seventeenth century   *H. 8.9 cm*
In 1693 John Dwight of Fulham brought a lawsuit for infringement of his 1684 patent for making red stoneware against the brothers John Philip and David Elers, who had come to England from Holland in about 1686. As a result John Philip Elers moved to Staffordshire, where he continued to make red stoneware until 1698. The crisp precision of this delicate teapot is very reminiscent of silver shapes, and since the brothers Elers had been silversmiths before becoming potters, it is almost certainly by them rather than Dwight. The decoration in the Chinoiserie manner is parallelled in many contemporary English productions of this date.   C.4–1932

Clock by Jeremie Gregory active from 1652,
d. 1685) 1685 *H. 66 cm W. 35.6 cm
D. 24 cm*
The monogram on the clock is a later
addition and can be interpreted as 'GEO: REX:
D:G:A:' for 'George by the grace of God the
King of England'. It seems probable that the
clock was in the Royal Collection during the
reign of George I (1714–27). The case and
mounts are exceptional for their architectural
character and complexity. The gilt bronze
group of Cupid on a Dolphin which forms
the finial is a refined version of a model
which exists in several examples, one being
in the Museum. They can be attributed to
Francesco Fanelli, who is known to have
worked in London between 1635 and 1642.
It may be supposed that his workshop survived the Civil War and was the source of the
finial and the other mounts on the clock.
Gregory, the clock maker, was Master of the
Clockmakers' Company in 1665 and 1676.
He also became a Goldsmith in 1668.

W.35–1976

◁
Staffordshire slipware dish *c.* 1675 *Diam. 43.8 cm*
The English slipware tradition involving decoration in a mixture of clay and water trailed on in lines and dots in the
manner of sugar-icing, or combed and feathered as on marbled paper, can be traced back to the Middle Ages. The finest
wares were made in North Staffordshire in the district now known as 'the Potteries'. This large dish belongs to a series,
signed by the potter Thomas Toft, some of which have dates between 1671 and 1677. The mermaid with her comb is
treated in a boldly simplified manner characteristic of the age, and the dish, like others bearing royal portraits and devices,
was evidently intended as a show piece for occasions of family ceremony.

299–1869

Duke and Duchess of Lauderdale by Sir Peter Lely (1618–80) *H. 137.2 cm W. 162.6 cm*

Lady Dysart, whose father William Murray had acquired Ham House in 1637, formed a relationship with the Earl of Lauderdale some time around the middle of the century, and after the death of their respective spouses, they married. Lely's oil portrait, which hangs at Ham House, clearly depicts the acute, politically minded, and rapacious aspects of the Countess's character, whereas her husband, whose ability and ambition had first attracted her, is shown only a few years before his death in 1682 when he was well past the zenith of his powers. The Lauderdales were among Lely's greatest patrons.

HH262–1948

The north drawing-room at Ham House *c.* 1637

Accounts for this room record that the plaster frieze and ceiling were made for £35.4s, the wainscoting for £5.10s, and the doors for £12 the pair, including door cases. The tapestries, depicting the seasons, can be dated between 1699 and 1719 and were woven by ex-Mortlake weavers. The chairs with their original upholstery were almost certainly in the room in the 1660s. The twisted columns flanking the fireplace are copied directly from one of the Raphael cartoons, which adds strength to the supposition that the room may have been designed by Francis Clein (see p. 48), who had used the cartoons at Mortlake.

The Melville bed *c. 1697   H. 462 cm   W. 243 cm   L. 274 cm*
This great bed made of pine and covered with silk damask and velvet is one of the few to have survived intact and in good condition from the last years of the seventeenth century. It belongs to the category of 'State Beds' which were designed, not necessarily for warmth or comfort, but to display the authority and wealth of their owner in a formal setting. The bed was commissioned by George, fourth Baron Melville and First Earl of Melville for the house at Monomail, renamed Melville, which he began in 1692. The design is probably based on those by Daniel Marot, some of which were published in his *Nouveaux Livres d'Apartements* in 1702, and the bed may have been made in London by the French immigrant craftsman François Lapierre.

W.35–1949

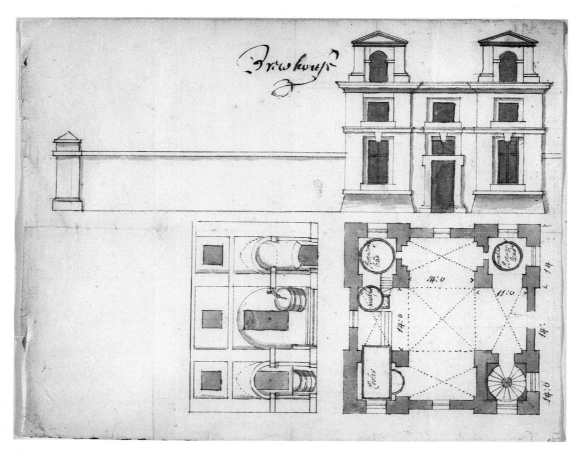

The brewhouse at Castle Howard *c.* 1700   *H. 21 cm W. 27 cm*
This drawing is one of forty-eight connected with the names of Wren, Hawksmoor, Vanbrugh, and their associates, previously owned by the Marquess of Bute, which the Museum acquired in 1951. They constitute part of a group which probably belonged to Christopher Wren junior and was sold in 1749 after his death. Castle Howard was designed by Sir John Vanbrugh (1664–1726) and Nicholas Hawksmoor (1661–1736) and built from 1699 for Lord Carlisle. In the design for the brewhouse as executed the towers project much further forward from the rest of the building and do not diminish in the attic storey as depicted here.
E.429–1951

Sketch for a recumbent effigy by William Stanton (1630–1705)   *c.* 1683   *L. 35.6 cm W. 12 cm*
This figure was originally thought to be a sketch for the monument of Isobel Shirburne at Mitton in Yorkshire by William Stanton the elder, but has since been unquestionably identified with the figure of Lady Rebecca Atkins (d. 1711) and her family, from the monument to Sir Richard Atkins (d. 1689) in St Paul's Church, Clapham by the same artist. Stanton's father and uncle were also sculptors, though their work is generally considered inferior. William Stanton is recorded to have completed at least thirty monuments in various churches throughout the country, including three in Westminster Abbey.
A.1–1929

Queen Mary II probably by John Nost the elder (d. 1729)   *c.* 1695
H. 59.7 cm
This painted terracotta statuette is probably the model for the statue
of Queen Mary by John Nost that was placed on the Royal Exchange
in 1695 after her death in December 1694. A companion statue of
William III was erected at the same time, the model for which is also
in the Museum (A.35–1939). Both statues vanished after the fire
which destroyed the Exchange in 1838. Nost was born on the
Continent but came to England and set up a workshop in the
Haymarket, where he employed many assistants. Vertue records that
he 'became a master of reputation and left behind him a good
fortune'.   A.208–1946

Wallpaper   Late seventeenth early eighteenth century   *H. 195 cm*
W. 60 cm
This detail of a strip of wallpaper made up from six separate pieces
came from Orde House, Berwick-on-Tweed, Northumberland. It is
printed from wood blocks and colour stencils and has been varnished.
The parakeets and Chinoiserie figures are evidence of the popularity
of Oriental subjects at this time brought about as a result of the
importation of Chinese and other goods by the Dutch East India
Companies.   E.5311–1958

Georgian and Regency (1715–1837)

The story of the arts in the eighteenth century is no longer one of Church and Court patronage, but one in which most of the important commissions came from the aristocracy and the middle classes. Furthermore, it is one of changes in style dictated to a certain extent by the tastes of these patrons. Thus, although the Baroque architecture of Wren, Vanbrugh, and others was already being criticized in the first decades of the century, it was Colen Campbell's *Vitruvius Britannicus*, which began publication in 1715, and more particularly Lord Burlington's employment of William Kent to design Chiswick House, which founded the Palladian style here in the mid 1720s.

Chiswick, in keeping with other Palladian houses, has an austere and dignified façade which contrasts strongly with its rich internal decorations. As the console table in Gallery 58 and other pieces make clear, part of this richness resulted from the retention of many Baroque forms within the new vocabulary of Palladianism. To a certain extent it was out of the flowing scrolls and curves of the Baroque and in reaction to the intrusion of classical formality in interiors that the Rococo style of the mid-century, with its delight in the fanciful and capricious, emerged. Chinese and Gothic forms, as well as the characteristic ornament derived from shell work—called *rocaille* in France where the style originated—were readily used by designers at this time.

No designer in Britain understood the Rococo idiom more fully, perhaps, than the furniture maker Matthias Lock, whose pattern books published in the 1740s were so influential. The mirror and side-table from the tapestry room at Hinton House in Somerset of *c.* 1745 which are displayed with Lock's original design in gallery 5 are splendid examples of his exceptional skill both as draughtsman and carver. Two other important contemporaneous furniture designers were John Linnell and his father William. The Chinese bed from Badminton House of *c.* 1755 which is now attributed to William, having being thought for many years to be the work of Chippendale, is perhaps the best-known piece of Rococo furniture in the Museum's collections. Among other interesting Rococo objects are the tapestry made at Soho in Gallery 58; the important group of ceramic Chinese musicians made at Chelsea in Gallery 123, which serves to remind us that it was at this time that Nicholas Sprimont introduced the art of making porcelain to Britain; and the pair of candlesticks by George Michael Moser, which illustrate the marked tendency towards assymetry exhibited during the Rococo period.

By the 1760s there were already signs of a return to more disciplined forms of ornament and decoration, and the greater study of the antiquities of Italy and Greece which were being undertaken by ever increasing numbers of Grand Tourists led inevitably to a concern with Neo-classicism. The discoveries made at Herculaneum and Pompeii; the architectural fragments and classical furniture in the Vatican Museum and the decoration of the Vatican itself; and classical monuments such as the Temple of the Winds and the Choragic monument of Lysikrates all provided models for new forms of ornament. Furthermore, the publication of several large volumes of engravings ensured that these sources were available to craftsmen and designers throughout the country.

Eighteenth-century Neo-classicism is usually referred to as the 'Adam' style after the architect Robert Adam, who was so widely patronized in the second half of the century. Osterley Park, the ceiling from David Garrick's villa at Hampton of 1770, the set of bookcases from Croome Court of *c.* 1763, and the panels from Northumberland House of *c.* 1773–4 constitute an impressive body of work by

Vertumnus and Pomona by Laurent Delvaux (1696–1778) *c.* 1725
H. 129.5 cm
This group illustrating Ovid's story of the wooing of Pomona by Vertumnus, a nature god who had the gift of transforming himself into any shape, was made while Delvaux was working in partnership with Peter Scheemakers. Along with a companion group of Apollo and Venus it was almost certainly made for Canons, the house which James Bridges, Duke of Chandos, built at Edgware. After the demolition of Canons in the mid-eighteenth century, the groups passed to Stowe where they remained until 1921. Delvaux was born in Flanders but came to England in 1721 with Scheemakers to work in Westminster Abbey with Denis Plumier on the tomb of John Sheffield, Duke of Buckingham. In 1728 he went to Rome, but returned to England in 1733 and remained here for a short time before returning to Flanders. Delvaux's treatment of drapery and the soft, rounded forms of his modelling are more Baroque than those of his contemporary Scheemakers. A.1–1949

Adam in the Museum and testify to his skill in manipulating a wide repertory of decorative and architectural motifs largely culled from Roman sources. Perhaps the most widely known of all Neo-classical objects are the 'basaltes' and 'jasperware' of Josiah Wedgwood, the master potter whose endeavours from 1754 were largely responsible for the successful expansion of the Staffordshire pottery industry. Amongst pieces of particular note by him are copies of the Portland Vase, and many portrait medallions designed by John Flaxman, whose sculpture is shown in the English Sculpture Court. Flaxman also designed for other manufacturers, such as Rundell and Bridge, whose silver is displayed in room 121.

Towards the end of the eighteenth century and throughout the Regency era Neo-classicism became increasingly concerned with accurate imitation and adaptation of antique models so as to ensure a firm basis for a universal criterion of good taste. This led to the rejection of Adam's simplicity and refinement in favour of more correct details and of greater opulence and exuberance of form. Supports for furniture in the form of animals, particularly lions, copied from articles found at Pompeii, for example, appear on several pieces of furniture in room 122, where a chair with a strongly curving arc-back and 'scimitar' legs which derives its form from fifth-century Greek vase paintings is also displayed. One of the most influential publications of the period was *Household Furniture and Decoration* (1807) by the wealthy connoisseur Thomas Hope, and the Museum is fortunate to have acquired several objects from his houses in Duchess Street, London and The Deepdene in Surrey. An Egyptian clock in gallery 121, which closely relates to one illustrated by Hope, is a reminder that Napoleon's Egyptian campaign in the early century added a further repertoire of archaic forms to the designer's stock in trade. But these sources were not English, and as the Industrial Revolution swept the country to world prominence, such considerations, as we shall see in the next chapter, became increasingly important.

Long case clock   *c.* 1725   *H. 266 cm W. 61 cm*
The clock is made of pinewood, japanned, with silvered finials and brackets, and the dial spandrels are filled with scrollwork ornaments of chased and gilt brass. The latter is inscribed with 'Markwick Londini' for James Markwick the younger.

W.49–1935

The Walpole salver   1728–9   *49 cm square*
This silver salver, which was probably engraved by William Hogarth (1697-1764), bears the maker's mark of Paul de Lamerie (1688–1751) and a London hallmark for 1728–9.   M.9–1956

George Frederick Handel (1685–1759) by Louis-François Roubiliac (1705?–62) 1738 *H. 135 cm*
This famous marble statue of Handel playing Apollo's lyre was commissioned by the impressario Jonathon Tyers whose bust, also by Roubiliac, is in the Museum, and placed in the Pleasure Gardens at Vauxhall in 1738. It remained there until about 1814 when it was removed by one of Tyers' descendants, and in 1854 it was acquired by the Sacred Harmonic Society. From about 1900, until its purchase by the Museum in 1965, the statue belonged to Novello and Company, the music publishers. The pedestal dates from the nineteenth century. A.3–1965

Model for the monument in Westminster Abbey to Sir Isaac Newton *c.* 1730 *H. 35.6 cm*
L. 52.7 cm W. 23 cm
The monument to Sir Isaac Newton in Westminster Abbey, and a similar one to the first Earl Stanhope, occupy a commanding position against the organ screen, facing the nave. As the screen was altered in the nineteenth century, the effect of the two monuments, which were designed by William Kent (1685–1748) and executed by John Michael Rysbrack (1694–1770) is now a good deal diminished. The terracotta model for the figure of Newton is in detail very close to the finished marble and must represent the final stage of the sculptor's conception. A.1–1938

Pew group *c. 1740* *H. 16 cm W. 17.3 cm*
It has been suggested that the famous Staffordshire pew groups of which this is an example may all be the work of Aaron Wood, who was born in 1717 and was apprenticed in 1731 to Dr Thomas Wedgwood. C.6–1975

Figure of a Heavy Dragoon *c. 1760* *H. 19.9 cm L. 11.7 cm*
A very similar Staffordshire, Astbury type, group in the British Museum of a Light Dragoon must date from after 1755, when light troops were added to some dragoon regiments, and it is on this evidence that the dating of this figure is based. C.124–1938

Settee seat cover *c. 1730* *W. 138.4 cm D. 52.3 cm*
Canvas, embroidered with wool and silk in tent and cross stitches with details in padded satin, overcast and cross stitches. The two scenes which fill the centre of the cover are taken from illustrations by William Kent to Gay's *Fables*, first published in 1727. T.473–1970

Cabinet on stand   *c. 1715   Cabinet H. 104 cm W. 91.4 cm D. 58.4 cm Stand H. 89 cm W. 122 cm D. 61 cm*
The cabinet is composed of four Japanese black lacquer panels set in an English aventurine lacquer framing. The stand of carved softwood covered with gilded gesso corresponds in design with a side-table by James Moore at Hampton Court Palace, except that the table bears the crowned cypher of George I at the central point of the apron in place of the cockleshell on the Museum's piece. Believed to have been part of the furnishings of George II's bedchamber, the cabinet was obtained as a perquisite of office by the 4th Earl of Rockford, first Lord of the Bedchamber and Groom of the Stole.   w.30–1958

Gilt console table designed by William Kent (1685–1748)   *c.* 1730   *H. 89 cm W. 70 cm D. 45.7 cm*
This table, one of a pair, the other of which is now in 'The Great Chamber' at Chatsworth, was designed by Kent in about 1727 to 1732 for Lord Burlington's villa at Chiswick. The two tables probably stood in the Gallery, flanking its Palladian window. The design, etched by Vardy, is Plate 40 in *Some Designs of Mr Inigo Jones and Mr William Kent*, published in 1744. Although many of the houses designed by Kent contain furniture attributed to him, documented pieces are extremely rare; the Museum's table bears two labels on its back, the one printed with the words 'Dining-room' and the other with the ink inscription 'Devonshire No 26', and as a similar label is on a side-table still at Chatsworth, its Chiswick provenance is secure. The table is among Kent's earliest experiments in furniture design, combining revived Palladian and Baroque motifs.

W.14–1971

68

William Augustus, Duke of Cumberland
by Sir Henry Cheere (1703–81) 1746–7
Height including pedestal 66 cm
Sir Henry Cheere was probably of Huguenot
extraction and was apprenticed to the
mason-sculptor, Robert Hartshorne. From
1729–33 he worked in partnership with
Peter Scheemakers's brother Henry, and
thereafter he worked on his own, obtaining
numerous commissions for statues and
busts, particularly from Oxford University.
This particular bust was for many years
catalogued as by an anonymous sculptor.
The recent discovery of an identical lead
bust belonging to Lord Brownlow, with
contemporary documentation, however, now
enables a positive attribution to be made.
Henry Cheere also executed a lead equestrian statue of the Duke for Cavendish
Square.   A.12–1947

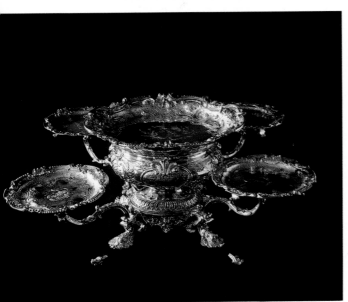

The Newdigate centrepiece by Paul de Lamerie (1688–
1751) 1743–4 *H. 23 cm W. 52 cm*
When the épergne began to come into use in about 1725, it
succeeded to the place of honour on the dinner table once occupied
by the great salt. The present example, which bears the London
hallmark for 1743–4, was made by Paul de Lamerie at his shop in
Gerrard Street, Soho, and the richness and fine finish of its
decoration are typical of the work with which his name is usually
associated.   M.149–1919

Centrepiece in the form of a tureen and cover by Nicholas
Sprimont (c. 1716–71) 1747 *H. 46.4 cm W. 67.3 cm*
The base of this silver centrepiece, which bears a London hallmark
for 1747 and the maker's mark of Nicholas Sprimont, is supported in
part by the cast and marbled armorials of John, 2nd Earl of
Ashburnham (1724–1812) and those of his wife. There are micro-
scopic traces of a different patterning at the edges of the cartouches,
which indicate that the piece was not commissioned by Ashburnham
but by another patron, also an Earl, whose arms were erased. M.46–1971

Mantua and petticoat *c. 1740*
This mantua and petticoat of crimson ribbed silk are embroidered with more than ten pounds of solid silver wire in a Baroque version of the oriental tree of life. A contemporary ink inscription below the embroidery on the underside of the train reads 'Rec'd of Mme Leconte by Me Magd Giles'. A Madame Leconte is listed as an embroideress in the accounts of Princesse Augusta in 1747, so that this dress was almost certainly intended for court use. It is the earliest signed dress in the world.

T.227 to B–1970

Bureau *c. 1745   H. 89 cm W. 157.5 cm D. 72.4 cm*
The terms 'Library Table', and 'Bureau Dressing Table' have been applied to pieces such as this, which were intended to be positioned in rooms, in pairs, back-to-back. The quality of workmanship helps to rank this piece among a small group of sumptuously produced furniture now attributed to the Exeter and London maker John Channon. The top drawer, which extends across the whole piece, is a writing drawer, and is supported on the corner trusses when pulled out.

W.4–1956

Printed cotton 1769 *L. 236 cm W. 190.5 cm*
Printed in a mixture of linen and cotton yarn from engraved copper plates, and overprinted from woodblocks. Both this scene and another depicting a shooting party, which is printed on the same piece of material, are signed R. JONES & CO. indicating that they were made by Robert Jones, who established an extensive calico-printing works at Old Ford on the right bank of the River Lea some time before 1761. Until he sold the firm in September 1780 Robert Jones and his artists produced some of the finest copper-plate chintzes ever made. Indeed, although printed cottons of this type are often called 'Toiles de Jouy' after the famous factory near Paris, cotton printing had flourished in England for many years previously. Engraved copper plates were used for printing cotton in England at least as early as 1757, whereas they did not come into use at Jouy until 1770 when they were proclaimed as a great discovery! T.140–1934

Pair of candlesticks   1740–5
H. 36.8 cm
In 1977 the Museum acquired two pairs of
unmarked silver candlesticks, each pair with
figures representing Apollo and Daphne.
The figure of Daphne resembles very closely
a drawing for a candlestick in the Museum
(E.4885–1968) signed by George Michael
Moser, R.A. (1706–83), the Swiss born
chaser and enameller who arrived in England *c.* 1721 and was to become a pioneer of
the Rococo style here.   M.329–1977

Chair   *c.* 1754
This ebonized beechwood chair is one of a
set of eight from Horace Walpole's Great
Parlour at Strawberry Hill, Twickenham. In
July 1754 Walpole planned the design of
some chairs, the backs of which were taller
than usual and were based on Gothic
window frames. Richard Bentley was employed to prepare the design and they were
made by William Hallet, who charged
£3.15.0 for each one in September 1755.
The set was sold at the Strawberry Hill sale
of 1842. Four chairs from the set are now in
the Lewis Walpole Library at Farmington,
Connecticut and two others in Bunratty
Castle, Ireland. This chair was formerly the
property of David and Lady Pamela
Hicks.   W.29–1979

Chelsea porcelain group of Chinese musicians   *c.* 1755   *H. 35.6 cm*
This porcelain group, which is marked with a red anchor and painted in enamel colours and gilt, can probably be identified as the 'large group of Chinese figures playing on music' which was lot 82 in the catalogue of the sale held by the Chelsea proprietors on 8 April 1756. Another example of the group is in the Untermeyer Collection in the Metropolitan Museum of Art in New York. The group was probably modelled by the Flemish artist Joseph Willems, who was responsible for so many of the figure groups introduced at Chelsea between 1749, or slightly earlier, and 1766.

C.40–1974

Design for a mausoleum for Frederick, Prince of Wales (1751–2) by
William Chambers (1723–96) *H. 32.4 cm W. 48.3 cm*
William Chambers' work at Kew commenced in September 1757 when he was
first commissioned by Augusta, Dowager Princess of Wales. During the course
of the next six years some twenty-five buildings and objects were erected there
to his designs, but now only five survive, of which the Orangery and the Pagoda
are perhaps the best known. This design was never executed. 3339

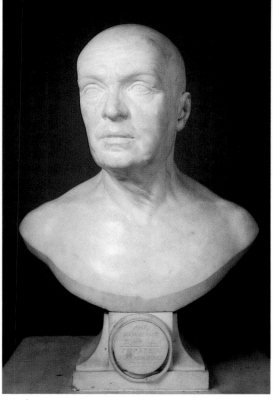

Dr Antonio Cocchi (1695–1758) by Joseph Wilton
(1722–1803) 1755 *H. 62.6 cm*
The bust was executed in the last year of Wilton's
residence in Italy. Cocchi was a celebrated Italian physi-
cian and scholar, who was an intimate friend of Horace
Mann, the British envoy in Florence. The unusual un-
draped form is evidence of Wilton's close study of Antique
busts. A.9–1966

Commode attributed to Pierre Langlois *c.* 1760 *H. 86.4 cm W. 132.7 cm*
D. 59.1 cm
Surprisingly little is known of Langlois, a French cabinet maker who had set up
business in London by 1759 and who produced during the 1760s a considerable
quantity of very high quality furniture. This commode is attributed to him on
the basis of its similarity to two documented commodes at Woburn Abbey and
the Metropolitan Museum of Art, New York. w.8–1967

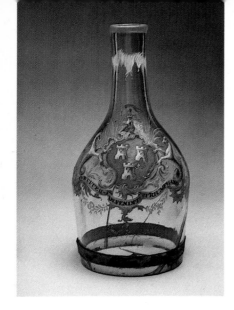

Glass decanter enamelled by William Beilby (1740–1819) 1762 *H. 23.5 cm*
The glass is painted in enamel colours and gilt and is signed 'Beilby Junr. Pinxit & Invt. NCastle'. The date 1762 has been added in diamond point. The coat of arms is that of Sir Edward Blackett, who was M.P. for Northumberland from 1768 to 1774.

C.620–1936

Urn and stand 1767–78 *H. 53.3 cm W. 33 cm*
Large, frequently silver, vessels such as this were used from the 1760s for preparing and serving tea. This example bears the mark of Thomas Whipham and Charles Wright, who were in partnership from 1757 to 1776.
Thomas Whipham was elected Warden of the Goldsmith's Company in 1772.

M.4–1918

Riding habit Mid-eighteenth century
This red cloth riding habit consists of a coat, waistcoat, and skirt. The buttons are covered with silver gimp and spangles, and floral embroidery, also in silver thread, gimp and spangles, is worked chiefly in satin stitch from the buttons and round the holes.

269 to 269C–1890

Armchair 1765 *H. 106.7 cm W. 77.5 cm D. 77.5 cm*
This gilded beechwood chair is known to have been made by Chippendale to Robert Adam's designs for the 'Salon' of Sir Lawrence Dundas's house at 19 Arlington Street, London. Contemporary records indicate that it was one of eight chairs for which he charged £160 in July 1765.

W.1–1937

Part of the glass drawing room from Northumberland House 1773–4

This room was designed by Robert Adam (1728–92) for Hugh (Smithson) Percy, 1st Duke of Northumberland, for his house near Trafalgar Square in London in 1773–4. The glass panels are backed with gilt metal foil to simulate the richness of porphyry and the overlay of Neo-classical motives are made of gilt metal, wood, and composition. The round and oval paintings were probably carried out by Giovanni Battista Cipriani, who is recorded as executing decorative painting at Northumberland House during this period. w.3-1955

Charlotte Walpole, Countess of Dysart by Sir Joshua Reynolds (1723–92) *c. 1775 H. 237.5 cm W. 146.1 cm*

The picture hangs in the great Hall at Ham House. When Lord Dysart died in 1727 he was succeeded by his grandson Lionel, the 4th Earl, who married Charlotte, the illegitimate daughter of Sir Edward Walpole, within a week of first meeting her. Charlotte died in 1789. Reynolds was one of the most esteemed portrait painters of his day; the flattering allusions to the Old Masters and to Antique sculpture which he cultivated in the poses of his figures appealed to the educated eye of the late eighteenth century. HH229-1948

The Kimbolton cabinet *c. 1771 H. 188.6 cm W. 177.8 cm*

This cabinet was designed by Robert Adam for the Duchess of Manchester, wife of the 4th Duke. It is mounted in ormolu, the wooden surface being of satinwood inlaid in darker wood with foliated arabesques and other classical motives, and faced with land and seascapes in coloured marbles (*pietre dure*) and the pilasters with strips of this material framed in brass. On the back of one of the panels is scratched the name of the maker 'Baccio Cappelli Fecit Anno 1709 Firenza', indicating that they were probably bought in Florence and sent home as curios. w.43-1949

The Duet by Arthur Devis (1711–87)   1749   *H. 115.6 cm W. 103.5 cm*
This oil painting with its great charm, cool delicate colour, and high finish is typical of Devis' small portraits and conversation pieces. Most of his patrons were solidly middle class and are usually portrayed in their gardens or parks, or, as here, in a sparse but carefully detailed interior, as if they had been assembled rather than grouped before the painter. His brother Anthony was a minor painter of landscapes and his son Arthur William a painter and draughtsman in the service of the East India Company.   P.31–1955

Vauxhall Gardens by Thomas Rowlandson (1756–1827)   *c.* 1784
H. 48.3 cm W. 74.9 cm
Rowlandson started as a painter of serious subjects but quickly
turned to cartoons. The Vauxhall Pleasure Gardens were opened in
1732 by Jonathon Tyers as a place of evening entertainment for the
summer months on a site across the Thames from the Tate Gallery.
Before their closure in the nineteenth century they provided anecdote
and incident galore in the novels, diaries, and letters of the time.
Many of the spectators depicted by Rowlandson have been identified.
They include Boswell, Dr Johnson, and Oliver Goldsmith, who are
seated beneath the box.   P.13–1967

Creamware teapot   *c.* 1775   *H. 11.4 cm*
Cream-coloured earthenware was first made by Enoch Booth of
Tunstall, and improved in 1765 by Wedgwood, who called his pottery
'Queen's ware'. This teapot was made at Leeds, one of several
potteries where Wedgwood's techniques were copied. The demise of
creamware was occasioned by the development of bone china in the
early nineteenth century.   C.99–1911

Dessert stand by Paul Storr (1771–1844)   1810–11
H. 33 cm W. 21.6 cm
Paul Storr is best known for the pieces of presentation plate so much
in demand as gifts to victorious generals and admirals during the
Napoleonic Wars, and for many no less successful but smaller
domestic pieces which he produced when working for Rundell and
Bridge from 1811–19, and in partnership with John Mortimer and
others from 1822. He retired in 1839. Two further versions of this
dessert stand formed part of the first Duke of Wellington's
Ambassador Service now at Apsley House.   M.40 A & B–1970

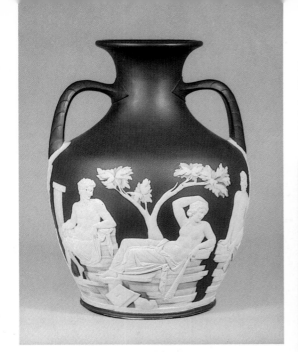

Facsimile copy of the Portland vase   1790–5   *H. 25 cm*
Diam. 18.4 cm
Wedgwood is recorded to have made between forty and fifty jasperware copies of the Portland vase (now in the British Museum), of
which only twenty or so are known to survive. This copy is said to
have been considered by Wedgwood himself as the most perfect of
them all.   Circ.732–1956

Henrietta, wife of the first Earl of Yarborough (d. 1813) by
Joseph Nollekens (1737–1823)   1810   *H. 64.8 cm*
Nollekens' able and lifelike busts ensured him a position in sculpture
almost equal to that of Reynolds in painting, and he died leaving a
fortune of some £200,000. He was, however, a very miserly man and
not liked by his pupils. One, J. T. Smith, ruthlessly delineated the
unpleasant aspects of his character in his biography *Nollekens and His
Times* and another, Joseph Bonomi, described him as 'that silly old
fool'.   A.120–1929

St Michael overcoming Satan by John Flaxman (1755–1826)
1822   *H. 90 cm W. 38 cm*
This plaster is the sketch model for the marble group which Flaxman
made for the 3rd Earl of Egremont between 1819 and 1826 and
which is now at Petworth House. The full-size model for the group is
on loan to the Museum from University College, London. It is one of
the sculptor's last works, and has links with Mannerist sculpture:
Benvenuto Cellini's 'Perseus', for example, which Flaxman had
studied in Italy.   312–1898

Pier table *c. 1800* *H. 91.4 cm W. 183 cm D. 48 cm*

This table of giltwood with bronze medallions was designed for the banker, patron, and collector Thomas Hope (1769–1831) for the 'Flaxman Room' at his house in Duchess Street, where it formed part of the elaborate setting for Flaxman's sculptoral group, *Cephalus and Aurora.* Hope described the table in his *Household Furniture and Interior Decoration* of 1807 as follows: 'Females emblematic of the four horae as parts of the day support its rail, the frieze of which contains medallions of the deities of night and sleep.' Such themes are representative of Hope's belief in the principle of symbolic and narrative ornament. The marble bust of 1790 is by Anne Seymour Damer (1749–1828) and represents Mrs Freeman as Isis. W.19–1976

Bookcase 1806 *H. 176.5 cm W. 112 cm D. 52 cm*

The bookcase is made of pollard Yew inlaid with ebony, and the mounts are of bronze and ormolu. It was supplied in 1806 by the firm of Marsh and Tatham of Mount Street, London for the Prince of Wales at Carlton House, and bears the inventory mark of George IV. A contemporary bill indicates that this was one of four similar pieces which Marsh and Tatham made for the sum of £680. Thomas Tatham was the brother of Charles Heathcote Tatham, and since the latter's name appears on some of the firm's bills dated 1806 it is possible that the bookcase may be to his designs. A writing desk made from fragments of furniture from Carlton House in 1835, with end panels bearing the same design as on the doors of the Museum's bookcase, is at Windsor. W.102–1978

Night lamp *c. 1820 H. 22.4 cm* ▷

The burner is contained within a porcelain turret-shaped stand in two parts with battlemented top. The piece was acquired as an example of a 'food warmer' of 'Nant-Garw' paste, but subsequently a drawing of the shape was discovered in one of the pattern books belonging to Messers Minton of Stoke on Trent, where it is described as a 'night lamp'.

C.601 to E–1935

Cup and saucer *c. 1810 Cup H. 7.2 cm Diam. 6.6 cm, Saucer Diam. 13.6 cm*

The decoration is painted in red enamel and gilded. A cup and saucer with this pattern in the Museum at Tunstall, where they were made, is ascribed on traditional grounds to William Adams, the potter who trained under Wedgwood, and much of whose subsequent work was equal to that of his master in quality. Apart from painted wares, Adams also produced transfer printed pieces, and cream and jasper wares.

II & a–1904

Cabinet *c. 1815 H. 113 cm W. 173 cm D. 56.5 cm*

The recent discovery of an album of tracings, which once belonged to the cabinetmaker George Bullock, in the Birmingham Museum and Art Gallery, has enabled this cabinet to be positively attributed to his workshop. Bullock started his career in Liverpool but moved to London in 1813. Apart from his cabinet making and upholstery work, he is also known to have been a sculptor and marble mason. Bullock's influence appears to have been extensive, for apart from his London and Liverpool commissions he also carried out work in Scotland for several wealthy clients, including Sir Walter Scott. The decoration along the bottom edge of the Museum's cabinet is very similar to that on two dwarf cabinets at Blair Castle, where he worked for the 4th Duke of Atholl.

W.32–1979

Satan arousing the Rebel Angels by William Blake (1757–1827)   1808   *H. 51.4 cm W. 39 cm*
This pen and water-colour painting is one of a series of illustrations which Blake made to John Milton's *Paradise Lost*. It illustrates the passage 'Awake! arise, or be for ever fallen' in which the fallen Satan summons the rebel angels to conference. Blake was concerned with illustrations for Milton's epic for more than fifteen years from 1801. This illustration is part of a series commissioned in 1808 by Thomas Butts.

The drawing shows Blake's linear, flatly-coloured style, which is typical of his work in the early years of the century, when he abandoned pictorial traditions in favour of a two-dimensional display of emblematic figures. Later his pictures were more highly finished and he applied the pigment in a broken technique to achieve an almost jewel-like finish.   6856 (FA 697)

Necklace Second quarter nineteenth century *L. 59.7 cm*
From about 1820 a fashion for naturalism pervaded all the applied
arts. At first confined to somewhat stylized designs, by the middle of
the century craftsmen attempted to reproduce natural forms as
accurately as possible. In jewellery the illusion of reality was made
more complete by mounting stones in the form of flowers on
'tremblers' so that they would shake at the slightest movement. This
necklace is made of gold of two colours set with seed pearls.

M.133–1951

Chair designed by Philip Hardwick (1792–1870) 1834
H. 81 cm W. 42 cm D. 40.6 cm
This carved, painted, and gilded beech chair was designed by
Hardwick for the Court Drawing Room at the Goldsmith's Hall and
made by W. & C. Wilkinson. Most of the suite of which it formed part
was destroyed during the Second World War when the hall was
bombed. This chair was salvaged, however, along with three others
which are still in the possession of the Company. Until his health
broke down in 1843, Hardwick maintained an extensive architectural
practice in London, and in 1854 received the Royal Gold Medal of
the Royal Institute of British Architects. The commission to design
the Goldsmith's Hall, which was carried out between 1829 and 1835,
included other furnishings besides this chair, and among the pieces
to his designs which survive are a fine set of mahogany dining chairs
in the 'Grecian' style.

W.1–1964

Bashaw by Matthew Cotes Wyatt (1777–1862) 1834
H. 149.4 cm including base
In 1831 Lord Dudley and Ward commissioned Wyatt to execute a
sculpted portrait of his favourite Newfoundland dog, Bashaw, which
was to be placed in his house in Park Lane. The dog was sent to
London from Himley Hall and 'sat' to Wyatt some fifty times. Lord
Dudley died in 1833, before the marble had been completed, and in
the following year a dispute about the commission and the price
(£5,000) arose between Wyatt and the Executors. The argument was
never settled, Bashaw remaining in the possession of the sculptor till
his death in 1862. Wyatt showed the sculpture at the Great
Exhibition of 1851 with the title 'The Faithful Friend of Man
Trampling Underfoot his most Insidious Enemy'. It is made of
coloured marbles with eyes of topaz and sardonyx. The snake is of
bronze with ruby eyes.

A.4–1960

Porcelain plate made at New Hall
c. 1810   *Diam. 20.6 cm*
After the failure of the Longton Hall factory
in 1760 no porcelain was, as far as is known,
made in Staffordshire until 1782, when a
group of potters who had acquired
Champion's patent for making hard paste
porcelain in the previous year, set up at
Tunstall and later at New Hall, Shelton.
Naïve, colourful, almost peasant designs
such as appear on this plate are characteristic
of the pottery in the early nineteenth century,
and represent a genuine alternative to the
more formal patterns used by factories tied
to classical fashions.   C.1285–1924

Silk gauze scarf or stole (detail)   Early
nineteenth century   *L. 225.6 cm W. 47.6 cm*
In the eighteenth century a large number of
Huguenots fleeing from persecution in their
own country settled in Spitalfields, where
they re-vitalized the silk weaving industry.
The Museum's collections include many
important silks and water-colour designs
from this period by Anna Maria Garthwaite
and others. In the nineteenth century the
industry suffered from French competition,
a shortage of raw silk, and a lack of organization and good design. Attempts were made to
remedy this situation, but the industry never
achieved its former prominence.   T.291–1965

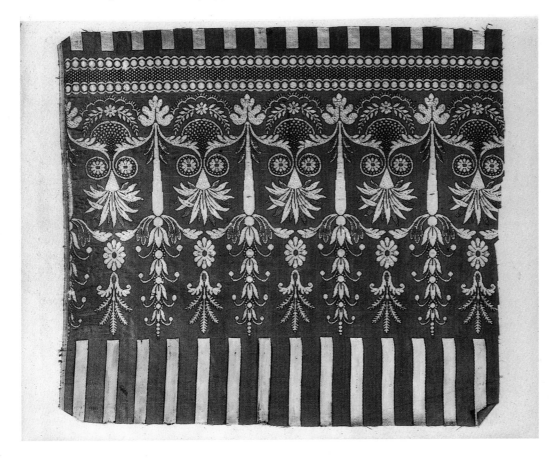

Caernarvon Castle by Peter De Wint (1784–1849)   *H. 30.5 cm W. 52 cm*
As a result of wise purchases and generous gifts and bequests, the Museum possesses a very rich and varied collection of the work of Peter de Wint, which is further strengthened by a permanent loan from the National Gallery. Although of Dutch descent, Peter de Wint was born in England. He won little reputation in his own day, although Constable realized his talent and occasionally purchased his work.

589–1892

East Cowes Castle, the Seat of J. Nash Esq.; the regatta starting for their moorings by Joseph Mallord William Turner (1775–1851)   *c.* 1828   *H. 91.4 cm W. 128.3 cm*
This oil painting, and a companion picture now in the Indianapolis Museum of Art, Indiana, were the direct result of a visit which Turner paid to the architect John Nash, who owned East Cowes Castle on the Isle of Wight, between July and September 1827. Nash set aside a special room in the castle for Turner's use.

FA 210

Stonehenge by John Constable   *c. 1835   H. 38 cm W. 59.7 cm*
Although Constable did not draw expressly as a preliminary to painting, this water-colour, which he exhibited at
the Royal Academy in 1836, was made in the previous year from a sketch of 1820. Into it he introduced the
rainbow which had fascinated him for more than twenty years as a symbol and embodiment of colour. Two
sketches for the water-colour are also in the Museum's collection.   1629–1888

Salisbury Cathedral from the Bishop's grounds by John Constable (1776–1837)   1820–3
H. 87.6 cm W. 111.8 cm
This painting, in oil on canvas, was commissioned in 1820 by Constable's friend John Fisher, Bishop of
Salisbury, who is depicted in the foreground with his wife. Constable was asked to alter the clouds and
was continually pressed to complete the picture.   FA.33

In a Shoreham garden by Samuel Palmer (1805–81)   *c. 1829*   *H. 28. cm W. 22.2 cm*
For some five years in the 1820's Palmer settled at Shoreham, in Kent, and here, amid surroundings of great pastoral luxuriance, he drew and painted many of the works from which his present-day fame chiefly derives. This water-colour sums up with great intensity Palmer's mystical feeling for exuberant nature in full bloom. Shortly before painting it, he had written of nature as 'sprinkled and showered with a thousand pretty eyes, and buds, and spires, and blossoms gemm'd with dew' and as containing 'rolling volumes and piled mountains of light'. The picture was purchased by the Museum from the artist's son in 1926.   P.32–1926

88

Victorian and Edwardian (1837–1910)

We have seen how earlier styles and the influence of exotic cultures have affected British art at various times since the sixteenth century. To suggest, therefore, that this was a uniquely Victorian process as has so often been done is not entirely accurate. What the Victorians did which was genuinely new was attempt to explain the nature and development of different styles in a logical and systematic manner. They hoped to deduce 'principles' from their historicist studies, and once the principles which motivated the ancients were understood they could be applied by artists, architects, and designers to put Victorian products on the same footing as those of the Greeks and the Goths. Thus, in surveying the somewhat bewildering collection of objects laid out in the Museum's Victorian and Edwardian primary galleries, one must not look simply for borrowed forms but for a genuine and original 'Victorian' style.

One of the first to write of such principles was the architect and designer Augustus Welby Northmore Pugin. His succinct advocacy of the Gothic style in various publications and his success in rebuilding the Houses of Parliament with Charles Barry after the disastrous fire of 1834 ensured a popularity for Gothic throughout the century. The Museum possesses several important pieces by him, including the large cabinet designed for J. G. Crace which was shown in the Great Exhibition of 1851, a desk from the Palace of Westminster, and various pieces of jewellery.

Interest in Gothic forms and decoration naturally led to a concern for medieval painted architecture and furniture. Most famous, perhaps, of the designers and architects who pursued this course was William Burges, whose best-known work is undoubtedly his rebuilding of Cardiff Castle and Castel Coch for the Marquess of Bute, between 1865 and 1875. The bed, wash-stand, and painted cabinet which he made for his own Tower House in Melbury Road, London show well his particular form of almost jocular medievalism. Among other important pieces of painted furniture are the large cabinet designed by Richard Norman Shaw and shown at the International Exhibition of 1862, and King René's Honeymoon cabinet designed by the architect John Pollard Seddon for his own use.

Another development of Gothic was the Arts and Crafts Movement championed by William Morris from the early 1860s. Morris devoted most of his life to the improvement of what he considered to be the debased standards of mid-Victorian mass production—a result of machine manufacture and the disappearance of hand craftsmanship. Although involved in the production of furniture and other three-dimensional objects, Morris's particular contribution to design was in the field of flat pattern making. Numerous books, wallpapers, printed and woven textiles, carpets, embroideries, and tapestries in the Museum's collections testify to the immense fertility and ingenuity of his imagination. He studied the different processes of manufacture in great detail not simply to facilitate production at the various workshops he set up but so as to ensure that his designs were appropriate to them. Morris's influence was so profound and far-reaching that few late nineteenth-century designers were unaffected by it. The Cotswold School, the name given to the various designers and cabinet makers including Ernest Gimson and Sidney Barnsley, who set up workshops in Gloucestershire, are perhaps the best known. Several examples of their elegant furniture and metalwork are on display; and particularly splendid is the cabinet made by Peter Waals, the experienced Dutch cabinet maker, who joined the School in 1901.

Contemporary with these developments in Gothic design and the crafts were those involving industrial manufacture. Morris's worries about the standards of design had, in fact, been voiced thirty years earlier by the Select Committee responsible for the foundation of the Schools of Design and the Museum. Sir Henry Cole himself set up Summerley's Art Manufactures to produce everyday articles designed by well-known painters and sculptors so as to 'promote public taste'. Most critics at this time were concerned about objects like the papier mâché tray (p.98), the ornamentation of which they did not consider appropriate. They held that patterns should be flat and disciplined and should not reproduce naturalistic forms faithfully.

The employment of designers in industry was not, of course, new, but it was undoubtedly given impetus by these developments. Most manufacturers requiring flat patterns turned at some time or another to architects and designers, and the number of tiles, wallpapers, carpets, and textiles in the Museum's collections which can be attributed to particular artists is prodigious. In the case of three-dimensional designs, those of Christopher Dresser for pottery and metalwork and Alfred Stevens for ironwork are outstanding.

By the 1890s a self-consciously 'new' decorative style was evolved, offering a lighter and more fanciful alternative to the rather academic and sombre 'aesthetic' taste of the 1870s and 1880s. Called Art Nouveau after a shop opened in Paris in 1895, it is characterized by limply swaying and curving forms, frequently stylized and naturalistic, and including female figures with long, flowing hair. Although many shallow relief and flat pattern designs in the Museum's collections, such as that by Archibald Knox for Liberty and Company, testify to the acceptance of the new style here, its more extreme forms were not as popular as on the continent. Similarly the work of Charles Rennie Mackintosh and the Glasgow School with its combinations of straight lines and gentle curves, frequently owing something to Celtic patterns, did not win the acceptance in Britain one might have expected. The furniture by the architect Charles Voysey typifies the more restrained forms favoured by English designers.

The Road to Capel Currig by John Sell Cotman (1782–1842) *H. 33.15 cm W. 43.8 cm*
John Sell Cotman was born in Norwich and spent the greater part of his working life there. Consequently, he is naturally associated with the Norwich School which flourished during the first decades of the nineteenth century. His true affinities, however, were much more with the new Romantic style of water-colour landscape typified by Girtin and the younger Turner, which he had studied at the house of the great patron, Dr Munro, in London. The rugged scenery of Wales, like that of Yorkshire, where he also travelled to paint, were consequently better fitted to his interests than the flat landscapes of East Anglia.   AL6860

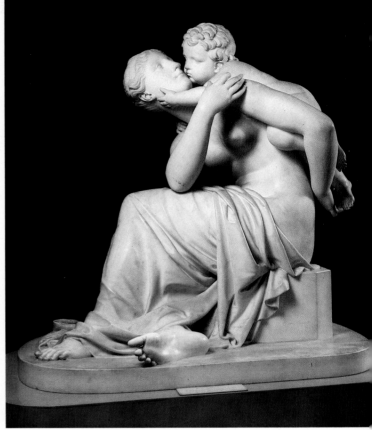

Maternal Affection by Edward Hodges Baily (1788–1867)
1837   *H. 94 cm L. 90 cm*
Although signed and dated 1837 Baily first conceived this group in
the early 1820s. He exhibited a plaster of it in 1823, and apparently
executed a marble in the following year. According to an entry in the
Art Union of 1847, this marble failed to sell and Baily eventually let
it go cheaply to Mr Neeld M.P. Since the Museum's group once
formed part of the Neeld Collection, and Baily did exhibit a group
under this title in 1837, the *Art Union*'s account, however, is not
wholly credible.   A.33–1964

Pandora by John Gibson (1790–1866)   *c.* 1856   *H. 172.7 cm*
Pandora was originally commissioned by the Duke of Wellington, but
Gibson did not carry out the work as the Duke had requested and he
declined to accept it. Gibson sold the figure instead to Lady Marion
Alford, of whom he remarked 'a lady of true knowledge in the arts,
and who had watched the progress of the statue with much interest in
Rome.... Lady Marion had become converted to polychromy, and I
therefore coloured the Pandora'. The Museum's uncoloured statue
is one of two marble copies which Gibson made.   A.3–1922

Tiara   First half of nineteenth century   *Diam. 19 cm*
The tiara, which is made of gold set with diamonds and pearls, is
composed of three parts. The large and small blossoms, made up of
numerous four-petalled flowers, possibly meant to represent a
hydrangea, date from about 1820. The two large sprays of oak leaves
with eight Baroque pearls as acorns date from about 1840, and the
single small blossom of conventionalized designs, set with large
diamonds, dates from the mid-nineteenth century.   M.117–1951

Cabinet bookcase designed by Augustus Welby Northmore Pugin
(1812–52)   *c.* 1851   *H.243 cm L.326 cm D.66 cm*
This carved oak cabinet bookcase which was made by J. G. Crace was
shown in the Medieval Court at the Great Exhibition of 1851.
Although the design resembles two bookcases illustrated in Pugin's
Gothic Furniture, published in 1835, it is closer in style to a drawing in
the Museum by Pugin dated 1849. Another drawing of the same date
for fittings for Crace's showroom in Wigmore Street, which incorporates an 'IC' monogram like that on the shields in this bookcase, may
indicate that Crace intended to include this piece in his showroom
after the exhibition. Other drawings for this bookcase are also in the
Department of Prints and Drawings, Paintings and Photographs.
The glass panes are a modern addition.   25–1852

Marriage jewellery designed by Augustus Welby Northmore Pugin
(1812–52)   1847–8
These pieces are part of a set of jewellery which Pugin designed in
anticipation of his marriage to Helen Lumsden. Already twice
widowed, Pugin had proposed to Helen in November 1847. She was
prevented from marrying by her family, however, and Pugin gave the
jewellery instead to Jane Knill, whom he married in August 1848.
The pieces were made by John Hardman and Company of Birmingham, whose account and day books record the precise dates of
manufacture and cost.   M.10, 20 and 21–1962

Manchester Town Hall by Alfred Waterhouse (1830–1905)   *c.* 1868   *H. 78.7 cm   W. 63.5 cm*
This is one of nineteen drawings which Waterhouse submitted in competition for the Town Hall in February 1868. Although he was placed fourth for 'architectural excellence', his designs were given first place for 'arrangment of plan and construction' and for 'economy and likelihood of being executed for the stipulated sum (£250,000)'. Furthermore, his design was said to be the best for 'natural light and ventilation' and he was declared the winner. The great hall, with its early English Gothic detailing and hammer beam roof, is decorated with wall paintings depicting scenes from Manchester history, which were carried out by Ford Madox Brown between 1876 and 1888.

D.1882–1908

93

Cabinet designed by William Burges (1827–81) 1858 *H. 213.4 cm W. 140 cm D. 38 cm*
This cabinet of painted and gilt wood was designed by Burges for H. G. Yatman and made by Harland and Fisher. The panels were painted by E. J. Poynter (1836–1919) and depict the story of Cadmus, the cutting of cuneiform letters, Dante and Caxton, and the heads of History, Poetry, Anaxagoras, and Pericles. The lower part of the cabinet draws out as a writing desk with two cupboards on either side. The gable roof and finials are derived from cupboards in Noyon and Bayeux cathedrals, and the dormers in the roof act as a calendar. The cabinet was exhibited in the International Exhibition of 1862. Apart from his furniture and metalwork designs, William Burges is best known for his architectural work, particularly Cardiff Castle and Castell Coch which he restored for Lord Bute. His own Tower House can be seen in Melbury Road, London. Circ.217–1961

Decanter designed by William Burges (1827–81) 1865 *H. 28 cm Diam. 17.8 cm*
The decanter is made up from a glass bottle mounted in chased and parcel gilt silver set with amethysts, opals, and other semi-precious stones and Greek and Roman coins. It is inscribed round the neck with the name of James Nicholson for whom Burges designed it, and the date 1865, and it bears the maker's mark of Richard A. Green. Burges had made two other very similar decanters for his own use out of the profits of his publications. Circ.857–1956

Table designed by George Edmund Street (1824–81) *c.* 1854 *H. 66 cm D. 98 cm*
This is one of a number of tables designed by Street for the students' bedrooms at Cuddesdon College. Although Street was much involved with the firm of Holland through his two wives Maraquita Proctor, who died in 1874, and Jessie Mary Anne Holland, who he married in 1876, it seems more likely that this table was made on site at Cuddesdon by local joiners. In style it is similar to the later productions of the Arts and Crafts Movement, and this is significant because Philip Webb who designed furniture for Morris and Company was working in Street's office at the time of the Cuddesdon commission. w.88–1975

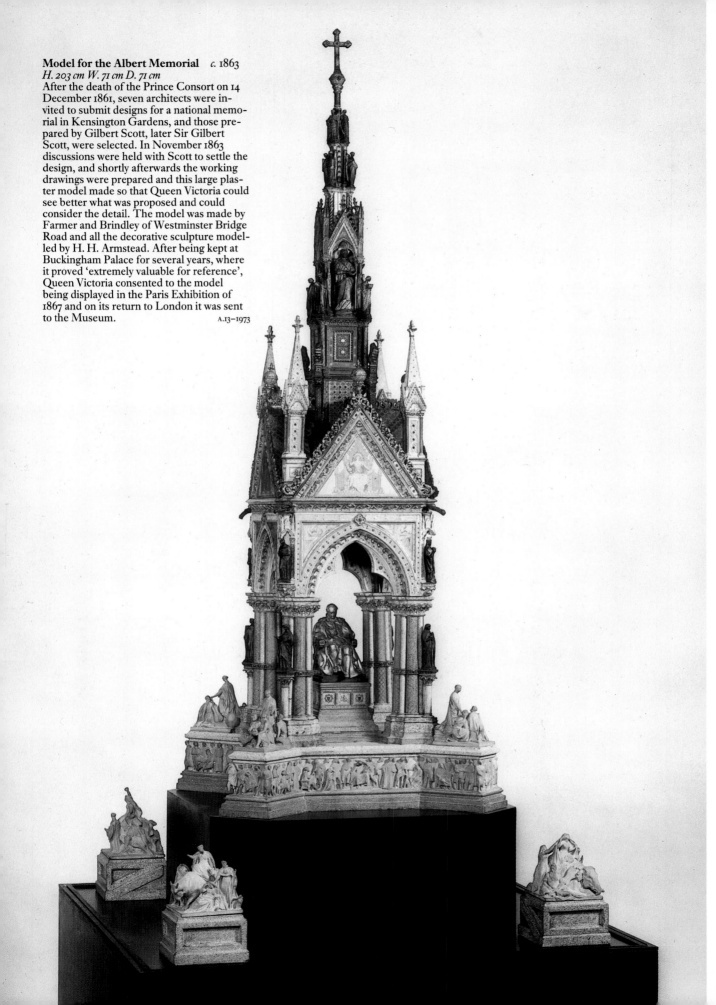

Model for the Albert Memorial   *c.* 1863
H. 203 cm W. 71 cm D. 71 cm
After the death of the Prince Consort on 14
December 1861, seven architects were invited to submit designs for a national memorial in Kensington Gardens, and those prepared by Gilbert Scott, later Sir Gilbert
Scott, were selected. In November 1863
discussions were held with Scott to settle the
design, and shortly afterwards the working
drawings were prepared and this large plaster model made so that Queen Victoria could
see better what was proposed and could
consider the detail. The model was made by
Farmer and Brindley of Westminster Bridge
Road and all the decorative sculpture modelled by H. H. Armstead. After being kept at
Buckingham Palace for several years, where
it proved 'extremely valuable for reference',
Queen Victoria consented to the model
being displayed in the Paris Exhibition of
1867 and on its return to London it was sent
to the Museum.   A.13–1973

Vase designed by Alfred Stevens (1817–75) 1864
H. 43 cm W. 23 cm
Among the advocates of the Renaissance, as opposed to
the Gothic revival of the last century, the most important was undoubtedly the sculptor Alfred Stevens.
This vase is one of several which were made to his
designs by Minton, Hollins & Co. 184–1864

Model for the Wellington monument in St Paul's Cathedral by
Alfred Stevens (1817–1875) 1857 *H. 197 cm W. 70 cm L. 98 cm*
The Wellington monument is probably Alfred Stevens' best-known
work. The story of its conception in 1857 when Stevens was at first
placed joint fifth in an international competition and its completion in
1912, after Steven's death, is one of the most scandalous, tragic, and
intriguing in English Art. Stevens' slow rate of working was at the
heart of the problem. The heroic figure groups of Truth and
Falsehood, and Valour and Cowardice had a great influence on the
succeeding generation of British sculptors. 44–1878

Hot air stove designed by Alfred Stevens (1817–75)
1850 *H. 127 cm W. 67 cm D. 91 cm*
Alfred Stevens prepared several designs for metalwork for the
Sheffield manufacturer Henry Hoole between 1850 and 1857. This
stove was one of a number of objects he designed specially for the
firm's stand at the Great Exhibition and which won for them a
Council Medal. Stevens' sympathy with metal and the casting
method, particularly with the sculptured qualities which could be
achieved, gained for the firm a reputation for fine products second to
none in the mid-nineteenth century. 4030–1853

Parlourmaid's tray   *c. 1865*   *L. 62 cm*
W. 45.7 cm
The tray, which is made of papier mâché, with
inlay of ormer and other shell is shaped for
carrying in front of a maid or waiter, the outer
rim convex and scalloped, and the inner
slightly concave and plain. Useful and decorative articles made of papier mâché have been
produced all over the world from early in the
Christian era and are still being made today.
Interestingly, the term, although French, was
probably first used in this country in the
seventeenth century. Perhaps the best-known
manufacturers are the Birmingham firm of
Jennens and Bettridge. It was their patent of
1847 for applying steam to papier mâché
panels to make them pliable which enabled
machines to be made for pressing and mould-
ing items such as this.   w.8–1959

Jacquard woven picture   *1862*   *H. 17.8 cm W. 10.2 cm*
The picture was woven by the Coventry firm of J. and J. Cash, now famous for the
manufacture of woven name tapes, for the International Exhibition held in
London in 1862. As a result of the Cobden Treaty in 1860, import duties were
removed from foreign ribbons which flooded the British market. Weavers in
Coventry, which was the centre of ribbon weaving in Britain, were forced to
abandon the manufacture of dress and furnishing ribbons for which there was no
longer a market, and many turned their looms instead to making pictures such as
this. In spite of this expedient, however, hundreds of firms were shut down. J. & J.
Cash and Thomas Stevens, famous for his Stevengraph pictures, were among the
few to survive.   T.90–1957

Room from The Grove, Harbourne, Birmingham 1877

This panelled 'boudoir' or ante-room designed by the Birmingham architect John Henry Chamberlain (1831–83) for William Kenrick (1831–1919) forms one of the most outstanding features in the Victorian Primary Galleries. Since it was originally used as the main entrance to the drawing room and was, consequently, kept free of furniture, Chamberlain was able to use more lavish decoration than elsewhere in the house. The resulting synthesis of Gothic forms combined with extreme naturalism, and here and there a hint of Japanese, particularly in the floral panels, owes as much to the teachings of Owen Jones as to those of Ruskin. The panelling, which is of sycamore and oak with inlay of walnut and other woods, was given to the Museum by the Kenrick family and Birmingham City Council when the house was demolished in 1963.

W.4–1964

Group of furniture by the Pre-Raphaelites *c.* 1860
The large oak cabinet against the wall on the right was designed by the architect John Pollard Seddon (1827–1906) as a desk and receptacle for his drawings and instruments. The painted panels on the front were contributed by his friends William Morris and Ford Madox Brown. In front of it stands an oak table designed in about 1860 by Philip Webb (1831–1915), architect of William Morris's Red House at Bexley Heath, and behind it against the wall on the left is a wardrobe which Webb also designed. This has painted panels by Edward Burne-Jones (1833–78) depicting scenes from Chaucer's 'Prioress's Tale', and was presented to William and Janey Morris as a wedding present.
Wardrobe: Ashmolean Loan.
Table: w.45–1926. Cabinet: w.10–1927

Page from a book of verse by William Morris (1834–96) 1870 *H. 27.9 cm W. 20.3 cm*
This book, which includes a selection of Morris's poetry expressing the fear and anguish of love, was given to Georgina Burne-Jones. The delicate watercolours are by Edward Burne-Jones, Fairfax Murray, and George Wardle, some to Morris's own designs.
L.131–1953

Stained glass designed by William Morris (1834–96) 1872–4 *H. 71 cm W. 43 cm*
This is one panel from a set of three depicting minstrels, which with a similar set depicting poets were given to the Museum by Morris's daughter May. The set was many times adapted, by the addition of wings, as Minstrel Angels for church windows. C.677–1923

Tapestry 'Angeli Laudantes' 1894 *H. 240.7 cm W. 204.5 cm*
This wool and silk tapestry on a cotton warp was made at William Morris's Merton Abbey works. The figures are taken from Sir Edward Burne-Jones's cartoon for the stained glass window which Morris & Co made for Salisbury Cathedral in 1879. The border and background were designed by John Henry Dearle who was director of the Merton Abbey tapestry works. Further copies of the tapestry were woven in 1898 and 1902, and in 1905 enlarged versions were made both of 'Angeli Laudantes' and a companion tapestry, 'Angeli Ministrantes', for Eton College Chapel. The Merton Abbey workshops by the River Wandle in Surrey were set up in 1881 when Morris & Co's premises at 26 Queen Square in Bloomsbury became too small. They continued to be used until 1940 when, rather than lower its standards because of the wartime conditions, the firm went into voluntary liquidation.   153–1898

Photograph of Isambard Kingdom Brunel (1806–59) by Robert Howlett (d. 1858)   November 1857   *H. 28 cm W. 23 cm*
This albumen print, of the engineer Brunel standing in front of the chains of one of the checking drums of his mammoth steamship the 'Great Eastern', is generally regarded to be one of the greatest masterpieces of 'environmental portraiture'. Although Howlett's short career was spent in the shadow of Joseph Cundall, one of the founders of The Photographic Club, which became the Royal Photographic Society in 1894, his series of 'Crimean Braves' photographed in 1856 by Royal Command established his importance as a photographer. In 1857 he took the photographs on which W. P. Frith based his famous painting of Derby Day.

246–1979

Evening dress *c.* 1894
This dress of midnight blue velvet trimmed with black jet and sequins was made in the United States of America by Stern Brothers of West 23rd Street, New York. It is included here both as an example of an evening dress of which the Museum has a large collection, but also because American dress and decorative art, of which there are also many examples in the collections of the Museum, do not fit rationally into the other volumes in this series. The necklace of silver and white pastes is English, *c.* 1840.   T.272 and A–1972

Harlequin and Columbine   Mid nineteenth century   *H. 33 cm W. 25.4 cm*
This print from the *Graphic* forms part of the enormous holding of theatre material given to the Museum by Mrs Gabrielle Enthoven in 1925. Along with many subsequent donations, it forms the basis of the Theatre Museum. At present the Museum's collections are housed in the Victoria and Albert Museum, but when the new Theatre Museum is completed in Covent Garden in the near future they will be moved there.

Soup tureen and ladle designed by Christopher Dresser (1834–1904)   1880   *H. 21.6 cm Diam. 23.5 cm L. of ladle 35 cm*
The electro-plated tureen and ladle are marked 'H & H 2123' and bear a registration mark for 28 July 1880. Dresser worked for the London and Birmingham silversmiths J. W. Hukin and J. T. Heath from about April 1878 for approximately three years, although the firm went on producing some of the designs until well into the present century. Dresser, a pupil of the Government Schools of Design, was much inspired by Owen Jones (1809–74), whose enthusiasm for scientific progress and belief in nature as an inspiration for design particularly appealed to him.   M.26–1972

A Halt in the Desert by John Frederick Lewis (1805–76)   1885   *H. 36.8 cm W. 49.8 cm*
Lewis was born into an artistic family, both his father and his uncle being artists. As a boy he studied animals with Landseer and many of his early exhibited works were of animal subjects. His predeliction for the Orient was apparently first stimulated by a visit to Granada between 1832–4. This inspired him to go to Cairo in 1841 where he lived for ten years. Many of his later paintings, such as this, were worked up from notes and sketches made during this time.

FA 532

Design for an exhibition building by Owen Jones (1809–74)   *c.* 1860   *H. 37.5 cm W. 72 cm*
Surprisingly little is known about Owen Jones, who was one of the most important architectural theorists of the last century. Almost all his buildings and decorative schemes have either been demolished or altered beyond recognition. This water-colour depicts one of three designs he prepared for a permanent industrial exhibition hall, winter garden, and pleasure park at St Cloud, near Paris, which was not built. The documentation of his involvement with the project is sparse and difficult to follow, but it is known that he was associated with Sir Joseph Paxton in the inception, and that the scheme grew out of their joint involvement with the Crystal Palace in Hyde Park and later at Sydenham.

D.946–1886

Sideboard designed by Edward William Godwin (1833–86) *c.* 1867 *H. 180.3 cm W. 259 cm D. 56 cm*
This sideboard of ebonized wood with silver plated fittings and inset panels of paper stamped in imitation of embossed leather was made to Godwin's designs by William Watt. Godwin was born in Bristol but moved to London in 1862. He was married for a time to the actress Ellen Terry, and was friendly with James McNeill Whistler, for whom he designed his most famous building, The White House in Tite Street, London, now demolished. The design of The White House, like this sideboard, reflects Godwin's great interest in Japanese art. Circ.38–1953

▽ **Vase and cover in the form of an owl** by the Martin Brothers 1899 *H. 26 cm Diam. 20 cm*
The Martin Brothers' pottery, active for more than three decades at Southall from 1877, was the joint enterprise of four talented brothers. Birds such as this were first made in the 1880s there by Robert Wallace Martin (1843–1923), who had a life-long love of humorous and grotesque ornament, inspired by stone carvings he carried out when working on the Houses of Parliament. C.491 and A–1919

Group of pottery by William Frend de Morgan (1839–1917) *c.* 1890 *Largest H. 23.8 cm*
The son of a mathematician and professor of philosophy, De Morgan was born in London and studied at the Royal Academy Schools. Ceramics were his main interest, however, and at various potteries in Fulham, Chelsea, and elsewhere he specialized in the production of wares such as these, which are obviously influenced by Near Eastern ornament. These pieces date from his Fulham period. C.421–1919, C.4–1905, 859–1905, Circ.193–1919
▷

Cabinet on stand 1902 *H. 188 cm W. 119 cm D. 48 cm*
This walnut and ebony cabinet with gilt gesso panels was designed by Ernest Gimson (1864–1919) and made at Daneway House, Sapperton in Gloucestershire, where he had set up workshops with Sidney Barnsley in 1902. Gimson himself executed the gesso panels but the remainder of the piece was made by Peter Waals, a Dutchman who before joining Gimson and Barnsley had had considerable experience of cabinet making on the Continent. The cabinet is illustrated as the frontispiece to *The Furniture and Joinery of Peter Waals* published by the Alcuin Press in 1930, and appears to have been one of the earliest pieces he made here. A design by Gimson for a similar cabinet, dated 1901, is in Cheltenham Museum and Art Gallery. This cabinet is remarkable for its radically innovatory form and proportions which anticipate developments in the 1920s. w.27–1977

Silver casket designed by Archibald Knox (1864–1933) for Liberty and Co. 1903 *H. 11.4 cm W. 21.8 cm D. 13.3 cm*
Archibald Knox was a native of the Isle of Man and began to work for Liberty's as a designer of silver, jewellery, and pewter in 1901 or 1902. He taught at the Kingston and Guildford Schools of Art and was also a water-colour artist and book illustrator. Many of his designs are in the Department of Prints and Drawings. This box is mounted with opals and bears a Birmingham hallmark for 1903–04, and the maker's mark of Liberty & Co. (Cymric) Ltd. M.15–1970

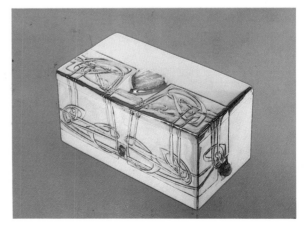

Queen Victoria by Sir Thomas Brock
(1847–1922) 1902 *H. 54.6 cm W. 38.7 cm
D. 25.4 cm*
After Queen Victoria's death in January 1901
a committee was appointed to consider what
form the National Memorial to her should
take. Several architects were invited to
submit designs for the replanning of the Mall
and the ground in front of Buckingham
Palace, and one sculptor, Thomas Brock, to
submit designs for a sculptural monument to
form the centre-piece of this scheme. Brock
was almost certainly chosen because he had
executed more statues and busts of the
Queen than any other living sculptor. This
bronze was cast by Singer of Frome, now
Morris Singer, from a model of his proposal
which was approved by King Edward in June
1902. A bronze cast from an earlier model
showing the complete monument with the
Queen surrounded by groups depicting
those virtues for which she was renowned is
also in the Museum. In execution few altera-
tions were made to this scheme and it was
unveiled on 16 May 1911, when Brock was
knighted. A.8–1977

Printed cotton 1902 *H. 86.4 cm
W. 61.6 cm*
This is one of a number of samples of
furnishing textiles which were taken from
ledgers in the possession of the firm of F.
Steiner and Company Limited of Accrington
at the time of its liquidation in 1957. The
design, which is a typical example of the
kinds of 'art nouveau' patterns which were
mass produced on textiles and wall papers at
this time, was registered at the Patent Office,
and consequently its date is known
precisely. T.128–1957

Writing desk and chair designed by Charles Francis Annesley Voysey (1857–1941) 1896 and 1909 *Desk H. 168 cm W. 84 cm D. (open) 87 cm, Chair H. 140 cm W. 64 cm*
The chair is made of oak, and is upholstered in leather. It is one of a set of twelve which Voysey designed in about 1909 for the offices of the Essex and Suffolk Equitable Insurance Company, Capel House, New Bond Street. A water-colour drawing in the Museum (E.711–1969) shows eight of the chairs arranged in the Company's board room with other furniture also designed by Voysey. The oak writing desk with copper hinges was designed for W. Ward Higgs Esq., and made by W. H. Tingey in about 1896. w.6–1953, Circ.517–1954

Hanging by Godfrey Blount (1859–1937) 1896 *H. 211 cm W. 180 cm*
The hanging, which was only recently acquired by the Museum, is made of variously coloured handwoven linens applied onto a natural coloured linen background. Godfrey Blount, who was educated at Winchester and Pembroke College, Cambridge, later studied art under Hubert Herkomer and at the Slade under Legros. His interests turned away from painting, however, and in 1896 he set up the Haslemere Peasant Industries, where this hanging was made, for weaving, embroidery, simple furniture, and other crafts. Later still he founded the Peasant Arts Society. T.173–1978

Chair and fireplace designed by Charles Rennie Mackintosh (1868–1928) c. 1900 *Chair H. 137 cm W. 49.5 cm D. 47 cm, Fireplace H. 152 cm W. 142 cm*
The chair was made for the Glasgow School of Art, Mackintosh's most famous building, and was exhibited at the Vienna Secession exhibition of 1900. The firegrate was made for the Willow Tea Rooms, also in Glasgow, in about 1904. The combination of straight and curved lines in Mackintosh's work provided a real alternative for British craftsmen to the more swirling and contorted forms of continental art nouveau, but was not as influential as might have been expected. Circ.130–1958, Circ.244–1963

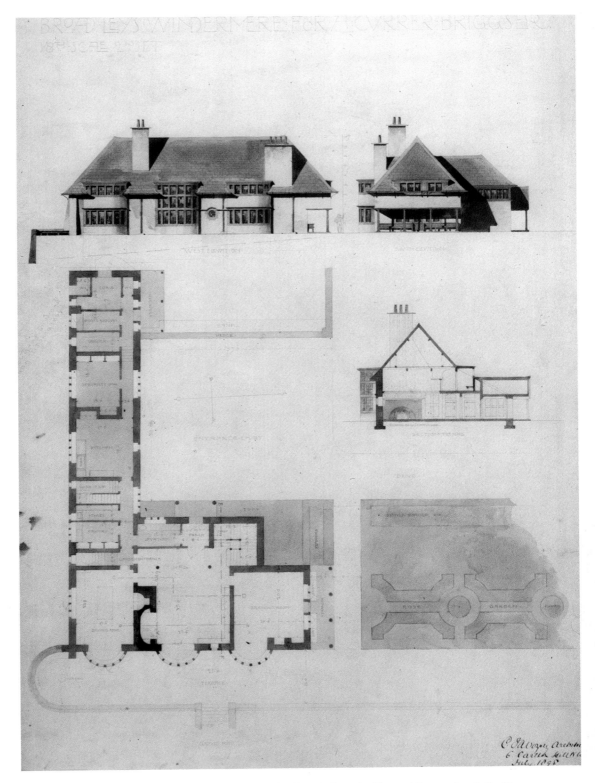

Design for Broadleys, Cartmel, Lancashire by Charles Francis Annesley Voysey (1857–1941) 1898 *H. 73.7 cm W. 52 cm*

Broadleys was one of several houses which Voysey designed for the Windermere area in 1898. All have steeply pitched roofs and wide eaves, and an austere severity which may reflect the harsh climate and barren landscape in which they were set. All Voysey's designs, unlike those of many of his contemporaries and predecessors, were structurally simple and relatively inexpensive to build. Contemporary accounts of a drawing of Broadleys which Voysey showed at the Royal Academy in 1899 notice that his style of draughtsmanship in pencil with 'whitey green' washes was something 'which Mr Voysey has invented'. It certainly marked a very distinct break with High Victorian architectural drawings and soon became the accepted mode among many of his contemporaries.

E.252–1913

THE ECONOMIST BUILDING

SCALE 1/16
E 6047
29 SEP 1960
13 DEC 1960
24 MAR 1961

ALISON AND PETER SMITHSON
46,
Limerston Street,
Chelsea,
London, S.W.10.
ARCHITECTS

AXONOMETRIC

The Twentieth Century (1910–the present)

Much of this chapter is concerned with the post-First World War period and its concern with industrial design rather than individual handcrafted objects. Before considering that, however, it is necessary to look briefly at the work of Roger Fry, the artist who was so passionately concerned to encourage the arts in Britain in the early years of the century. It was Fry who organized the exhibition in 1910 of 'Manet and the Post Impressionists' which so stimulated British artists, and resulted in Eric Gill, Wyndham Lewis, Stanley Spencer, Duncan Grant, and others showing alongside Picasso, Braque, and Matisse in a second exhibition in 1912.

Fry's importance in the field of the decorative arts lies in his founding of the Omega Workshops in 1913, a studio where objects of everyday use were designed and decorated with bold patterns in Post-Impressionist colours. Many objects made in the workshops are now shown in the twentieth-century study collections: wooden candlesticks painted by Duncan Grant; an embroidered footstool designed by Fry and worked by Mrs Bartle Grant; a marquetry tray depicting Wrestlers designed by Henri Gaudier Brzeska; and a ceramic stove with tiles painted by Duncan Grant and Vanessa Bell. Among post-War objects made in the workshops is a wooden frame with embroidered panels by Mary Hogarth after designs by Wyndham Tryon of c. 1923. In the context of most other pieces of furniture in the Museum they appear somewhat amateur and rather exaggeratedly brash, but they do, nevertheless, possess a strength both physical and artistic, and an originality which contrasts strongly with the often excessively attenuated, structurally weak forms of Art Nouveau.

Roger Fry's concern with public standards of taste and the spirit of working together which the First World War encouraged both contributed to a generally felt desire to improve standards of design in British industry after 1918. The Design and Industries Association and 'Fitness for Purpose' grew up out of the Arts and Crafts movement with its emphasis on work by individuals and its belief in the rural tradition. The result of this, in the early 1920s at least, was to encourage the production of objects of simple form such as could be made by existing machinery from traditional materials. The best-known examples in the Museum's collections, perhaps, are the pieces of furniture by Sir Ambrose Heal, whose shop in Tottenham Court Road did so much to foster good design at this time, and those by Gordon Russell.

But while the members of the D.I.A. were concerned with pursuing this somewhat nationalistic course, new and exciting innovations were being made on the Continent, particularly in Scandinavia and at the Bauhaus in Germany. International Modernism, with its emphasis on structural and formal rationalism and its concern with new materials, made its first strong impact here with the exhibition of modern French and English furniture which Serge Chermayeff organized at Waring and Gillows in 1928. Some British artists were already familiar with the idiom, most notably the Irish designer Eileen Gray, whose superb lacquer screen was made as early as 1923. But she had lived in Paris for many years: to those resident in Britain Chermayeff's clear statement of what constituted honest twentieth-century design was a revelation. Numerous V & A objects were shown in the recent 'Thirties' exhibition organized by the Arts Council, and many are now on display in the twentieth-century study collections. They include a chromed steel standard lamp by the architect Oliver Hill of 1934; a pair of glass stands and a mirrored screen designed by Syrie Maugham, Somerset Maugham's wife, in 1935; laminated wooden furniture designed by

Economist centre by Peter and Alison Smithson c. 1960 *H. 73 cm W. 44.8 cm*
In 1959 The Economist newspaper arranged a limited competition for designs for a new building to house its offices, a bank, and some residential accommodation. Later, the site was enlarged when it agreed with the proprietors of Boodles that new Club premises would be included in the scheme too. The competition was won by the Smithsons, whose design was much praised, particularly for its sympathetic treatment of the difficult site. By designing three quite separate blocks and keeping the smallest on a line with St James Street, the centre is made to harmonize very successfully with the surrounding buildings. The project was completed in 1965.
Circ.376–1974

Marcel Breuer for Isokon, the firm set up in 1931 to put into production the design concepts of Wells Coates and Jack Pritchard; a dining table and chairs designed by Eric Ravilious in 1936; tubular steel chairs by P.E.L. Ltd; carpets by Marion Dorn and Betty Joel; pottery by Keith Murray and Susie Cooper; the extraordinarily original furniture designed by Denham Maclaren as early as 1931; and best known of all, perhaps, the entrance foyer of the Strand Palace Hotel designed by Oliver Bernhard between 1929 and 1930.

Just as the D.I.A. and Modernism had grown out of the First World War, so the Council of Industrial Design and utility grew out of the Second. The Utility Furniture committee was set up soon after November 1942 and the Council in December two years later. Gordon Russell was very influential on both. But after the gloomy War years utility was not popular. Designers and public alike felt the need for something lighter and more frivolous, and two important exhibitions, 'Britain Can Make It', held in the Victoria and Albert Museum in 1946, and the Festival of Britain in 1951 provided exactly the opportunity that was required to indulge this taste. Both had very far-reaching effects on British design, not only because so many designers participated in staging them, frequently without any of the usual shackles imposed by anxious manufacturers, but also because they involved larger numbers of the public than had been reached since the Great Exhibition a century before.

The Museum's recent 'A Tonic to the Nation' exhibition documented the Festival of Britain and its influence fully, and included many objects from the collections: Robert Gooden's silver tea service made for the Royal Pavilion at Brighton; formica with designs derived from molecular structures by the Festival Pattern Group; and furniture designed by Ernest Race and Lesley Dunn, to name but a few. These objects, like Robert Heritage's 'Hamilton' sideboard designed for Archie Shine Ltd., and Robin Day's work for Hille later in the decade, have an undeniably 50s character, 'not exactly stark but not exactly cosy' as one writer has put it. By the mid 1960s such generalizations were quite impossible, for design quite suddenly veered in several directions at once as Op and Pop and other styles quickly succeeded each other. Even the concept of permanence was brought into question as products were deliberately designed to be disposable. Terence Conran's Habitat shops had perhaps the most widespread influence, particularly on middle-class interiors, with their promotion of 'basic' objects owing as much to rustic cultures as to those of 'advanced' society.

In the 1970s the dominant theme may well prove to have been the revival of the crafts. Certainly John Makepeace's column of drawers, Roger Doyle's clock, Jacqueline Poncelet's bowls, Archie Brennan's tapestry, and Rupert Williamson's chair are all elegant witnesses of a move away from industrialism. Like Habitat's involvement with scrubbed pine and peasant weaves this is appropriate, for the applied arts have always reflected developments in technology, and in the 1970s scientists developed for the first time alternative technology as seriously as its conventional counterpart.

North Wind stone sculpture by (Arthur) Eric (Rowton) Gill (1882–1940) *c.* 1928 *H. 25.4 cm L. 69 cm D. 11.4 cm*

Although most famous, perhaps, for his calligraphic and other printed work, Eric Gill also carried out many sculptural commissions. The best known are probably the Stations of the Cross which he carved between 1913–18 for Westminster Cathedral, decorative sculpture for the exterior of Broadcasting House, of which North Wind was a part, and similar work for the League of Nations Building in Geneva in 1936. His sculpture is characterized by the same crispness and flatness so evident in his typographic work. Although he was made a Royal Designer for Industry in 1936, throughout his life Gill was much involved with hand as opposed to industrial production. After conversion to Roman Catholicism in 1913, he took part in the formation of the Guild of St Joseph and St Dominic, a semi-religious community of craftsmen; in 1920 he was a founder member of the society of Wood Engravers; and in 1928 he set up his own printing press at Speen in Buckinghamshire. A.10–1942

Book illustration by Edmund Dulac
(1882–1953) 1911 *H. 31.8 cm W. 25.4 cm*
Edmund Dulac was born in Toulouse. After
two years of training for a legal profession he
gave this up and moved to Paris, where he
studied art at the Academie Julian. Already
an Anglophile and deeply interested in book
illustration, he emigrated to England in 1904
and became a British subject in 1912. This
pen and ink and water-colour drawing was
for an illustration of 'The Snow Queen' on
page 51 of *Stories from Hans Anderson*
published by Messrs Hodder and Stoughton
in 1911; it depicts the sentence '"It is gold,
it is gold!" they cried.' E.392–1948

The Eclipse of the Sunflower by Paul
Nash (1889–1946) 1945 *H. 42 cm
W. 57 cm*
Paul Nash was educated at Chelsea Poly-
technic and the Slade, and held his first one
man exhibition at the Carfax Gallery in 1912.
He served in the First World War at the
front before being appointed an Official War
Artist in 1917. He was again appointed in the
Second World War, at the end of which this
picture was painted. It reveals both the poetic
and surreal aspects of his work. He had
earlier been rather stimulated by Surrealism
and exhibited with the Surrealists in their
Paris Exhibition of 1938. An oil version of
this picture is in the collection of the British
Council. Nash also did much work as a
designer and book illustrator, and both these
aspects of his work are well represented in
the Museum's collections. P.19–1962

Writing table   1925   *H. 107.7 cm*
W. 135 cm D. 52 cm
Designed by (Sir) Edward Maufe, this writing table of gilded mahogany, camphor wood, and ebony, gessoed and faced with white gold, was made by W. Rowcliffe and shown at the Paris Exhibition of 1925. Although Maufe designed furniture and other appplied arts he is best known as an architect, his most famous commission being Guildford Cathedral, which he won in open competition in 1932.   Circ.898–1968

Lacquer screen designed by Eileen Gray (1879–1976)   1923   *H. 207 cm*
Eileen Gray was born in County Wexford, Ireland but moved to London to study at the Slade in 1898. It was while she was there that she learned the technique of making oriental lacquer in the shop of D. Charles in Dean Street which she happened upon one day in her lunch break. In 1902 she moved to Paris and not long after met and began to work with Sugawara, a Japanese master of Lacquer. It was not surprising, therefore, that when in 1922 she opened a gallery in Paris called Jean Desert, lacquer objects such as this screen should have featured among the exhibits. Because of the time involved in their production, however, such objects were very expensive and few were made and sold.   w.40–1977

Wardrobe decorated by the Omega Workshops   1916   *H. 173 cm W. 157.5 cm D. 45 cm*
In 1913 Roger Fry (1886–1934) opened a communal artistic workshop with Duncan Grant and Vanessa Bell, which he called the Omega Workshops. Fry was intent on applying the decorative qualities of Post-Impressionist Art to works of domestic utility so as to elevate general taste. They were obliged to close in 1919, however, partly for financial reasons but also because the participants were artists and consequently lacked enthusiasm for their roles as decorators. This wardrobe is said to have been part of a suite of furniture designed by Fry for Madame Lala Vanderville.   Circ.272–1975

Design for Fisher's restaurant by
Raymond McGrath (1903–77)
1932   *H. 22.7 cm W. 35 cm*
Like Serge Chermayeff, Raymond
McGrath, who was born in Australia and
educated at Sydney University, came to
modern architecture by way of his interior
design work in the new style of the late
1920s. A chance meeting with Mansfield
Forbes, the Cambridge Univeristy don, resulted in the commission to remodel the
interior of 'Finella', Forbes' Regency House.
McGrath received much publicity for the
work, which he carried out in coloured
glasses and copper and green and pink paint,
and other commissions quickly followed,
including this restaurant in New Bond
Street, now demolished.   Circ.564–1974

Rug designed by Serge Chermayeff (b.
1900)   1930   *L. 152 cm W. 140 cm*
Chermayeff was born in the Caucasus, but
came to England in 1910 and remained here
until 1939 when he emigrated to the U.S.A.
During his time in this country he was a
director of Waring and Gillow's 'Modern Art
Studio' and a member of the influential Mars
Group with Eric Mendelsohn. For much of
this time he was also in private practise. It is
possible that this rug may have been made
for his own use. Certainly, very similar
carpets appear in illustrations of his house in
The Studio in 1930.   T.157–1938

Pendant Brooch by George Hunt *c.* 1935 *H. 8.9 cm W. 6.7 cm*
The brooch is made of gold and silver, decorated with ivory, enamel, mother of pearl, rubies, pearls, and tourmaline. It was shown at the Royal Academy in 1935 by George Hunt, the Birmingham jeweller and designer whose mark is stamped on the back. Egyptian influence has pervaded western art and design since before the Christian era. Napoleon's Egyptian campaign in the early nineteenth century and Howard Carter's opening of Tutenkhamen's tomb in 1924 have both been responsible for particular Egyptian fashions, however, which have affected the design of everything from clothes to biscuit tins. M.41–1971

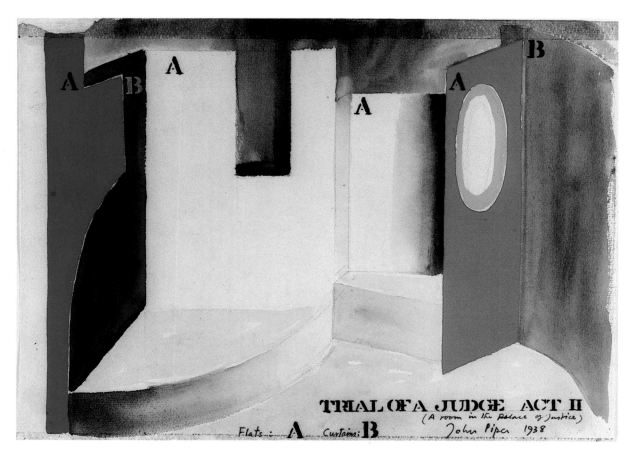

Design for a stage set by John Piper (b.
1903)   *c.* 1938   *H. 23.5 cm W. 32 cm*
The design depicts a room in the Palace of
Justice from Act II, Scene I of *Trial of a
Judge, A Tragedy in Verse* by Stephen Spen-
der. Piper, who studied at the Royal College
of Art from 1928–9, is best known for his
paintings and stained glass designs at Coventry and Liverpool Cathedrals. He has, however, designed various sets and costumes for
the stage, particularly for Benjamin Britten's
operas *Rape of Lucretia* in 1946, *Albert Herring*
in 1947, and *Billy Budd* in 1951.   E.79–1967

Printed cotton by Marion Dorn (1899–
1964)   1938   *H. 183 cm W. 127 cm*
Marion Dorn was born in San Francisco and
came to England in the early twenties. She
was eventually persuaded to move back to
the U.S.A. in 1940 but in the intervening
period she established a reputation here as
one of the leading textile and carpet designers. After an exhibition of hand-knotted
rugs in 1929 with E. McKnight Kauffer, she
received numerous commissions for textiles
and carpets for domestic interiors, hotels,
and liners. This particular printed cotton
entitled 'Exotique' was designed for Messrs
Donald Bros.   Circ.282–1938

Farmyard tapestry by Edward Bawden (b. 1903)   1950   *H. 167.6 cm W. 134.6 cm*
Bawden studied at the Cambridge School of Art from 1919 and at the Design School of the Royal College of Art where Paul Nash was a tutor from 1922–5. Although known primarily as a mural painter and illustrator, he has also designed earthenware for Wedgwood, tile decorations for London Transport's Victoria Line, wallpapers on which he experimented with John Aldridge, and textiles for the Orient Steam Navigation Co. Ltd. The tapestry was woven by the Edinburgh Tapestry Company Ltd. in their Dovecote Studios at Corstorphine, and reflects Bawden's love of rural life in Essex. Contented cows, for example, such as appear in a group at the top, re-appear frequently in his mural and graphic work.

T.273–1978

Seated Mother and Child by Henry Moore
(b. 1898)   1975   *H. 50.4 cm W. 38.3 cm*
Henry Moore is the most eminent living
British sculptor. He was trained in Leeds,
where he met Barbara Hepworth, and in
London before travelling to Paris and Italy in
1925. His earliest major work was the
'North Wind' (1928) for London Transport,
and his international reputation dates from
1948 when he was awarded the sculpture
prize at the Venice Biennale. This print was
made to be issued as a gift with the 125
copies of the Deluxe edition of the catalogue
raisonné of Moore's graphic work published
in 1976.   E.1422–1976

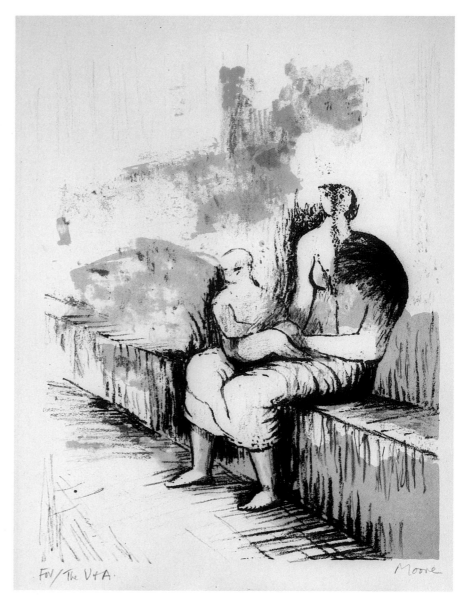

Nude girl, bronze by Frank Dobson (1888–1963)
H. 123 cm
Frank Dobson was the son of a Christmas card illustrator
and studied painting at the City and Guilds College,
Kennington. He took up sculpture after completing war
service in 1918 and was the only sculptor to exhibit in the
group X exhibition of 1920. Although best known for his
sculpture, he also designed and printed his own textiles
including batiks and lino blocks. Another example of his
sculpture is to be seen in the tiles he designed for
Goodhart-Rendel's Hays Wharf, on the Embankment.
                                              A.32–1971

Dark Island, textile hanging by Archie
Brennan 1971 *H. 172.7 cm W. 99 cm*
Archie Brennan trained at the Dovecot
studios in Scotland before he went to art
school and returned in 1963 to become a
Director. It was there that he learnt the skills
of tapestry weaving which have stood him in
such good stead. Many of his tapestries take
the form of visual jokes and would not
succeed but for his great technical skill.
Some of the effects he incorporates are the
result of mistakes which he deliberately
works into the designs, and it has been said
of him that the 'risk-taking, real life quality'
of weaving 'is the thing he really loves'.

Circ.331–1973

Stoneware vases by Bernard Leach (1887–
1979) 1963 *Larger H. 28.6 cm D. 19 cm*
Bernard Leach, until his recent death, was
the leading figure in the development of
studio pottery in this country. He first discovered pottery when living in Japan between
1909 and 1920, and after returning to this
country set up his own studio with Shoji
Hamada at St Ives in Cornwall. From that
time until he stopped pottery in 1972 as a
result of failing eyesight, he held regular
exhibitions of his work, taught and lectured
frequently, particularly at Dartington Hall in
Devon, and wrote numerous books. During
the 50 years or so that he potted, Leach's
style changed surprisingly little. The influence on him of Japan, and also of Korea
which he visited on a second trip to Japan, is
always apparent. It is interesting that his
work has always been much respected by the
Japanese, who in 1966 awarded him The
Order of the Sacred Treasure, second
class. Circ.551–1963, 1192–1967

Chair by Rupert Williamson (b. 1945)
1976   *H. 96.5 cm W. 48.3 cm D. 50.8 cm*
The chair, which is of maple and rosewood with a
leather seat, was made by Rupert Williamson while
he was a student at the Royal College of Art. After
leaving the college, Williamson worked for a short
while in two reproduction and restoration busi-
nesses before setting up with the aid of a grant from
the Crafts Advisory Committee in his mother's
house at Milton Keynes. He admits to being
uncertain about the derivation of his ideas, stating
in an interview with *Harpers and Queen* in 1978:
'people always put me in the class of Art Deco, and
it's true that I did look to the Twenties, because I
never liked the Sixties international style and I
didn't like the Fifties stuff either. I don't like
William Morris much or the Bauhaus, which is
what the Sixties were all about. At college I was
more interested in Celtic work than anything. I like
clean pieces like Biedermeir; although I didn't
discover the existence of Biedermeier until two
years ago, they use woods like I use them.' At the
same time he admitted to being 'Really . . . a
sculptor, making functional things . . . what I want to
make is exclusive, decorative objects'.   w.18–1977

Bone China bowls by Jacqueline Poncelet
(b. 1947)   1972 and 1976
Larger H. 8.9 cm D. 13.3 cm
Jacqueline Poncelet, a student of the Royal
College of Art, made her first pieces in
stoneware. After finding that she was doing
more and more carving, however, she turned
to bone china quite naturally as a much more
responsive vehicle for this type of technique.
She casts all her pieces to begin with and
then proceeds to carve their surfaces, sometimes spending as long as two days whittling
away at a single piece. The later of these two
bowls was made in the St Pancras workshop
she set up with Glenys Barton, a fellow Royal
College student, who also works in bone
china.   Circ.256–1976, 255–1976

Design for a new casino at Monte Carlo 1970 *H. 64 cm W. 87 cm*
This is one of a number of drawings and collages which were submitted by Archigram Architects for the competition arranged by the 'Societé des Bains de Mer' at Monte Carlo for a new summer casino and club in 1970. Archigram, which consisted at the time of Peter Cook, Dennis Crompton, and Ron Herron, won the competition, but although building was begun it was not completed when the project fell through in 1973. Circ.470–1974

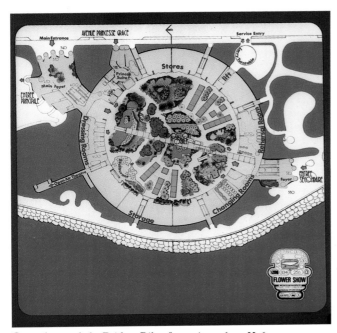

Gouache study by Bridget Riley (b. 1931) 1969 *H. 62 cm W. 98 cm*
This is a study for the emulsion on canvas painting 'Byzantium' which Riley completed in 1969. The identity of each red stripe is shifted by the band it encloses, and the white stripes, which appear to expand as they move outwards, are suffused with a delicate colour spread from the adjacent reds. The painting developed from a green and magenta canvas closely related to the 'Chant' series completed in 1967. Circ.663–1971

Man running towards a bit of blue by David Hockney (b. 1937) 1963 *H. 63.5 cm W. 52 cm*
This drawing was made at the time Hockney made his first excited visit to California and shows his early interest in painting water. Not only was the idea of depicting moving water in a very slow and careful manner appealing to him, but he was also impressed by the athleticism of young American men and painted at least one figure from photographs taken by the Athletic Model Guild, a group of Los Angeles photographers who specialized in studies of the male nude. Circ.298–1963

Bowl by Michael Lloyd (b. 1950) 1975 *H. 5 cm W. 9 cm*
Michael Lloyd graduated from the Royal College of Art in 1976. He says of himself 'I never sit down to draw the shapes, I just raise the silver until I feel that I've arrived at the correct shape for the design then I paint it white all over and draw the design on in pencil. I look at it for a few days while I work something else, maybe sketching. Only then I go back and see if its really what I want it to be, design and bowl an integral whole. My mind works incredibly slowly, and raising and chasing silver proceeds at just that same pace. That's why I like it.' Lloyd has made his home on a canal long boat and admits a debt to William Morris and Art Nouveau metalwork, particularly the work of Gaudi and Omar Ramsden. M.250–1977

Collar 1968 *L. 36 cm*
The work of the London jeweller Anthony Hawkesley, who designed and made this silver gilt collar, played a prominent part in the revival of the crafts in the 1960s. In the 1970s this revival was, perhaps, the most significant development in the area of the applied arts and was reflected in the establishment of the Crafts Council in its own right instead of as a Committee of the Design Council. M.25–1973

Dragon-fly clock by Roger Doyle (b. 1947) 1977 *Diam. 10 cm*

After leaving the Central School of Design, Roger Doyle served a five-year apprenticeship with Cartier Ltd. In 1969 he worked for Louis Osman on the crown used by Prince Charles for his investiture as Prince of Wales, and in the same year he set up his own workshop in London. This clock was specially designed for one of the series of Jubilee Masterpiece exhibitions organized in the Museum by Lady Casson in 1977.

M.126 & a–1978

Industrial pottery 1977

This pottery is from the 'Concept' range which Martin Hunt of the Royal College of Art and Colin Rawson designed for Hornsea Pottery in Yorkshire in 1977. It is made of vitramic stoneware, unglazed except on the interiors of all the receptacles, which are glazed. In style the design harks back to Art Deco which underwent a period of popularity at this time.

C.207 to K–1977

Column of drawers by John Makepeace (b. 1939)   1978   *H. 131 cm W. 51 cm*
John Makepiece first set up a furniture workshop at Banbury in Oxfordshire which flourished
and in 1977 he moved to larger premises at Parnham House, Beaminster, Dorset, where he
was also able to instigate a residential course for student craftsmen. 'We expect that at the end
of two years each student will have learnt all the basic skills and techniques of working with
wood, and will have built up his own clientele and begun to have developed an individual style
so that he is completely ready to set up and successfully run his own workshop.' Makepeace
understands well the business needs of the modern craftsman and has ensured that this is a
vital part of the course. This column of drawers, the depth of each drawer indicated by a
coloured band at its base, is one of a number of objects in different media which the Museum
has recently commissioned from contemporary craftsmen, in continuance, in point of fact, of
the traditions of the Museum when it was first founded. It represents a development on a
rather similar column of drawers which Makepeace showed at the Craftsman's Art exhibition
held in the Museum in 1973.   W.56–1978

Index